The Irish to the Rescue

The Tercentenary of the Polish Princess Clementina's Escape

Richard K. Maher (Ed.)

Peter Lang

Oxford · Bern · Berlin · Bruxelles · New York · Wien

Bibliographic information published by Die Deutsche Nationalbibliothek
Die Deutsche Nationalbibliothek lists this publication in the Deutsche Nationalbiblio-
grafie; detailed bibliographic data is available on the Internet at http://dnb.d-nb.de.

A catalogue record for this book is available from the British Library.

Library of Congress Cataloging-in-Publication Data
Names: The Irish to the Rescue: The Tercentenary of the
  Polish Princess Clementina's Escape (2019 : Europe House, Dublin) | Maher, Richard
  K., 1984- editor.
Title: The Irish to the rescue : the tercentenary of the Polish Princess
  Clementina's escape / Richard K. Maher.
Other titles: Tercentenary of the Polish Princess Clementina's escape
Description: Oxford ; New York : Peter Lang, 2021. | Includes
  bibliographical references and index.
Identifiers: LCCN 2020040854 (print) | LCCN 2020040855 (ebook) | ISBN
  9781789979329 (paperback) | ISBN 9781789979336 (ebook) | ISBN
  9781789979343 (epub) | ISBN 9781789979350 (mobi)
Subjects: LCSH: Maria Clementina, Princess, consort of James, Prince of
  Wales, 1702-1735--Congresses. | Marriages of royalty and nobility--Great
  Britain--History--18th century--Congresses. | James, Prince of Wales,
  1688-1766--Marriage--Congresses. | Maria Clementina, Princess, consort
  of James, Prince of Wales, 1702-1735--Kidnapping--Congresses. |
  Europe--Politics and government--1648-1789--Congresses. |
  Princesses--Great Britain--Biography--Congresses.
Classification: LCC DA814.A4 I75 2019 (print) | LCC DA814.A4 (ebook) |
  DDC 942.07092 [B]--dc23
LC record available at https://lccn.loc.gov/2020040854
LC ebook record available at https://lccn.loc.gov/2020040855

Cover design by Brian Melville for Peter Lang.

ISBN 978-1-78997-932-9 (print) • eISBN 978-1-78997-933-6 (ePDF)
ISBN 978-1-78997-934-3 (ePub) • ISBN 978-1-78997-935-0 (mobi)

© Peter Lang Group AG 2021

Published by Peter Lang Ltd, International Academic Publishers,
52 St Giles, Oxford, OX1 3LU, United Kingdom
oxford@peterlang.com, www.peterlang.com

Richard K. Maher has asserted his right under the Copyright, Designs and Patents Act,
1988, to be identified as Editor of this Work.

This publication has been peer reviewed to the highest international academic
standards.

Contents

Illustrations

✳

Antonio David, after Martin van Meytens, *Queen Clementina*, 1725, 73.2 x 61 cm, oil on canvas (Pininski Foundation, Liechtenstein). There are many copies and miniatures of this portrait, including this one painted by Antonio David in 1730. It was never engraved, but it was reproduced in mosaic in St Peter's Basilica in Rome, where it still forms part of Queen Clementina's funerary monument.

Polish Ambassador's Note

Dear Readers,

The dynamic pace of contemporary politics oftentimes results in an immersion in the present based on the assumption that the challenges and the opportunities we face are unprecedented in our common European history. Therefore it is so the more refreshing and intellectually enlightening to undertake an exercise of looking back to events which transcended borders, involved royals and exiles, gave insight into the role women play in politics, and resulted in heart-stopping adventure exactly 300 years ago.

I am delighted the three centuries' old story of the Polish Princess Clementina Sobieska's elopement, with the help of an Irish soldier of fortune, and marriage to the Jacobite claimant to the thrones of Britain and Ireland, James Francis Edward Stuart, has been revived, retold and is being collected in a book form for generations to come. It is a story where courage, beauty and strong characters played a role and shaped European history.

The commemoration of this 300 years' old story also merits attention as it reminds contemporaries that the Sobieski royal family was a symbol and proof of the strength and greatness of *Rzeczpospolita*. The story of the unconventional and beautiful princess Clementina Sobieska, who achieved her goal with the support of a rescue party of Irish people and a French aide, is one that symbolises the truly international roots of European history as well as the affinity between the Polish and the Irish, their willingness to join forces for the greater good.

This book itself is a result of exemplary transnational cooperation. The commitment of the editor and the contribution of all authors should be recognised.

Ambassador of the Republic of Poland to Ireland
H. E. Anna Sochańska

Acknowledgments

Both the seminar and this publication have received crucial financial support from the Polish Embassy in Dublin without which it would have been impossible to succeed. I extend especial thanks and profound gratitude to Dr Galia Chimiak who was Cultural and Media Affairs Officer at the Polish Embassy in Dublin, for her interest, advice and unstinting support to ensure the seminar and the follow-on publication were realised. I also wish to thank Dr Łukasz Chimiak who was Chargé d'Affaires of the Republic of Poland in Ireland for his support for both projects.

Both the seminar and this publication were also financially supported by the French Embassy in Dublin and I extend my thanks to its wonderful staff, Dr Marc Daumas, Science Attaché, and also to Ms Louise Aupetit who was very helpful in the planning and organisation of the seminar. I would like to thank Ms Christine Weld from the Alliance Française in Dublin who was also very helpful in preparation for the seminar. For his attendance on the day of the seminar, I thank H. E. Mr Stéphan Crouzat, Ambassador of the Republic of France to Ireland.

The editor wishes to sincerely thank Uachtarán na hÉireann - the President of Ireland, H. E. Michael D. Higgins for his interest in and attendance at the public seminar held on 30 April 2019 to commemorate Princess Clementina's rescue and escape. I also extend thanks to Mrs Sabina Higgins who expressed support for the seminar.

I acknowledge the very generous financial assistance offered by Principal Bernadette Moore and Deputy Principal Anna Morris of Rathmines College of Further Education which allowed the proceedings of the seminar to be recorded and published via podcast on the History Hub website. I thank them both for their support for the projects and for their attendance on the day of the seminar.

Dublin City Council kindly funded the tea, coffee and biscuits which were supplied at the interval during the seminar, and which were very much appreciated by both audience and academic participants.

I give hearty thanks to my friend Gary Dolan at Print Stations Ltd who supplied all printed materials to an excellent standard. The materials were used in the promotion of the seminar and were displayed and shared on the day itself.

I share my sincere appreciation for the staff of Europe House in Dublin who very kindly offered us the use of their main conference room *gratis*. This allowed us to move our plans forward rapidly.

I acknowledge an offer of help from the Technological University of Dublin for accommodation for one of the academic participants for which I am most grateful.

It has been my utmost pleasure to work with the academic participants of the seminar in April 2019, who are now contributing to this publication. They delivered excellent papers on the day of the seminar and generated huge interest in it. I am particularly indebted to Dr Declan Downey for his constant support and advice, and I wish now to express to him my profound gratitude for his professional guidance and his friendship over the past number of years. I sincerely thank Professor Edward Corp for his provision and explanation of the portraits of Queen Clementina used in this publication.

The National Museum of Neiborów and Arkadia, a branch of the National Museum in Warsaw, very kindly allowed us to use the portrait of Maria Kazimiera *gratis* and for that I thank them. I also express thanks to the staff at the Museum of King Jan III's Palace at Wilanów who helped me identify and obtain permission to use some of the images used here. For other images used here, the editor extends his thanks to the National Gallery of Ireland, the National Museum of Ireland, and the National Galleries of Scotland for their professionalism and their courtesy in providing me with some of the images contained in this book. For supplying an image at short notice I wish to thank the Vienna Museum.

I thank the staff of the National Library of Ireland who have always been helpful and courteous during my visits there. I give special thanks to Ms Anne-Marie McInerney, a librarian of Dublin City Library & Archive on Pearse Street in Dublin, who assisted me on an important reference check by telephone.

Finally, I extend sincere thanks to my mother Mrs Patricia Maher who helped to proof-read all of the contributions.

MARY ANN LYONS

Introduction

It has all the elements of a swashbuckling adventure. It is 1719 and all over
Europe, from Ireland to Russia, loyal supporters of the House of Stuart
(Jacobites) are feverishly engaged in all manner of intrigue and complex conspiracy aimed at restoring their exiled monarch, James Francis
Edward Stuart (James III) to the kingdoms of Britain and Ireland.
Seeking a bride for his exiled master, an Irish Jacobite officer named
Charles Wogan travels incognito throughout central Europe and finally
reaches Ohlau, residence of the illustrious Sobieski family. There he meets
the beautiful young royal Polish Princess Maria Clementina Sobieska
whose father agrees to the match. However, the reigning king of Britain
and Ireland, George I, fearing that the marriage will produce a new generation of rival Stuart claimants to the throne, persuades the Holy Roman
Emperor Charles VI to have the young princess arrested while en route to
the Italian states to marry her prince: she is confined against her will in
Innsbruck, deep within imperial territory. But then, having obtained the
secret approval of both Maria Clementina and her father Prince James
Louis, the heroic Jacobite officer, together with his companions, defies
logistics and atrocious weather conditions, snatches the princess from
her captors and spirits her away on treacherous mountain roads across
the Alps to safety in Bologna. The couple are finally united and marry
in Montefiascone, north of Rome, in September 1719. Afterwards, the
newlyweds take up residence in Rome at the special invitation of Pope
Clement XI who recognises them as King and Queen of Great Britain

and Ireland. In gratitude for saving his goddaughter, the pope offers to bestow the honour of senator of Rome on Wogan who accepts on condition that the same be given to his companions. One of the most celebrated great escape sagas of European history, this has it all: intrigue, rivalry and connivance among royals; secrecy and concealed identities; near tragedy; triumphant heroism; and a happy ending ... it seemed.

For the first time, the circumstances surrounding the episode have been the subject of close scrutiny by a range of scholars with expertise in Jacobite history, Irish émigré networks, court studies, material culture, the Habsburg-Hanoverian alliance and the Irish in Habsburg territories, Polish dynastic and political history, and musicology. Their complementary investigations featured in these eight essays lend significant dimensionality to this already fascinating story by framing the interpretation of the dramatised narrative within the cut and thrust of *realpolitik* in 1719 and the years that followed, thereby making it all the more real and compelling.

Richard Maher recounts in lively detail the dramatic tale in an essay which forms the centrepiece of this collection whose publication marks the tercentenary of the rescue of Princess Maria Clementina. It is to the protagonist, the Irish Jacobite officer, Sir Charles Wogan, that we are indebted for the colourful account of how the Irish came to the rescue of the princess which he recorded in a memoire of his titled *Mémoires sur l'enterprise d'Inspruck en 1719* [*Memoires of the Innsbruck Adventure of 1719*], which he wrote, dedicated and presented to Queen Marie Leszczyńska of France, cousin of Queen Clementina, in Paris on 4 March 1745. By that stage, Queen Clementina had died, as had his companion-kinsmen from Dillon's Regiment, leaving Wogan as the only person with detailed first-hand knowledge of the whole affair.

For Wogan the affair was a highlight in the distinguished history of the Irish Jacobite brigades. It is fitting, therefore, that this collection opens with an essay focusing on Wogan's place in Jacobite circles and on the loyalties, networks, machinations and aspirations of Irish Jacobite military exiles in Europe from the 1690s to the late 1740s. Éamonn Ó Ciardha sets the scene for the event in 1719 by situating it in the context of successive failed plots and invasion scares (1692, 1695, 1708, 1715, 1719, 1745 and 1759) in which loyal Irish Jacobites, including Wogan, looked to their exiled king,

and especially to their exiled aristocracy and gentry serving in the armies
of France and Spain, to achieve their own repatriation, restitution of their
lands, titles and dignities, and rehabilitation of their proscribed church.
Constantly alert to Europe's numerous dynastic wars and colonial, military
and political rivalries, mindful of their possible implications for a Stuart
restoration, this burgeoning Irish military diaspora actively participated
in abortive Jacobite military campaigns, invasion plots, cross-channel espionage and Irish Brigade recruitment-drives. As Ó Ciardha explains, their
frequently fraught activities in the realms of diplomacy, espionage, politics
and especially warfare testify to their cultural fluidity, mobility and vulnerability, and highlight the need to balance loyalty to the Stuarts with
political and military duty to the Bourbons and Habsburgs. Sir Charles
Wogan is presented as 'rebel', prisoner, fugitive, agent, diplomat, soldier
and statesman – the personification of the loyalty, romance and tenacity
that often characterised the Irish Jacobite émigré on a pan-European stage
that extended from his native Kildare, through the north of England,
to France, the Papal States, the Baltic, Russia, Spain and north Africa.
His spectacular intervention to preserve the Stuart royal dynasty in 1719
added lustre to his family's glowing reputation as loyal supporters of the
Stuarts and won him international recognition. Having secured Maria
Clementina's arrival in the Papal States, he became the talk and toast
of Europe. Pope Clement XI made him a senator of Rome, while King
James III gave him a knighthood, baronetcy, and a colonel's commission.
When viewed within the context of Jacobite history, it becomes clear why
Wogan's audacious rescue confounded Europe and delighted his Jacobite
contemporaries, thereby boosting both the Jacobite cause and the illus-
trious reputation of the fighting Irish abroad.

Complementing Ó Ciardha's exposition of the Jacobite context,
Declan Downey focuses on the villain in the drama, the Holy Roman
Emperor Charles VI. The reasons for Charles' amicable relationship with
King George I are effectively elucidated within the wider sphere of contemporary European power-equilibrium politics. This not only resulted
in Charles' detention of Maria Clementina; it also influenced attitudes
at the Imperial Habsburg Court towards the Jacobite cause and the nuanced responses among the Irish in the Austrian Habsburg establishment.

The importance of the timing of this dramatic episode in spring 1719, at a critical point in the War of Quadruple Alliance (1718–1720) when British naval support for Austrian forces in Sicily was vital, is also highlighted.

Narrowing the focus to the Sobieski dynasty, Jaroslaw Pietrzak traces their rise to prominence through military prowess and strategic marriage alliances from their late medieval origins to the end of their noble lineage in the eighteenth century, shedding valuable light upon the family's pressurised circumstances in the 1710s. Pietrzak paints a bleak picture. The wealth of King Jan III Sobieski was by then a myth, and the family were reduced to pawns in the European political arena. Viewed in the context of highly complicated negotiations around advantageous marriages for Prince Jakub's daughters, the blow dealt by George I and Charles VI's opposition to Maria Clementina's relationship with the Stuart pretender is shown to have compounded the Sobieskis' difficulties.

While the rescue of Maria Clementina ended happily for the couple and was celebrated by their supporters, what followed was far from a fairy-tale ending for them; the same was true for Sir Charles Wogan. The fascinating if tragic sequel, in which factional intrigues once again intruded upon their lives, is recounted in essays by Richard Maher and Edward Corp.

As Corp explains in his study of Clementina's life at the Jacobite court in Rome, although the marriage produced two Stuart princes, Charles, Prince of Wales (the future Bonnie Prince Charlie), and Henry, Duke of York (the future Cardinal York), it was, otherwise, a complete failure. Clementina was beautiful, popular and full of enthusiasm when she travelled from Silesia and escaped from Innsbruck to be married in Italy. However, six years after the wedding, she informed her father that throughout that time, she had been neglected and scorned, and had endured a kind of living death. Corp details how her life was ruined by her husband's three Scottish Protestant favourites and how she ended her days as a recluse within the Palazzo del Rè where she devoted herself almost entirely to her Catholic religion, apparently became anorexic, and died when she was just 33 years old. Particularly fascinating is the analysis of Clementina's depiction in portraits. Corp compares the first, executed by Francesco Trevisani in the spring of 1719, shortly after her arrival in Rome, in which the 17-year-old princess looks radiantly beautiful and is portrayed as the Queen of England, with several others commissioned by James III during the 1720s. He then contrasts these with three from the early 1730s in which she appears thin, wearing her ermine lined blue cloak over a simple dress, her hair combed back into a simple bun. Corp's discussion of Clementina's weight loss, and her determination to use her 1727 portrait in which she appears thin, modestly dressed and holding a breviary to publicise how badly she was being treated and to bargain for the dismissal of the three Scottish favourites from the Jacobite court provides a fascinating insight into this young woman's strategies for demonstrating her agency and protest at her maltreatment.

In his essay on Wogan's service and exile, Richard Maher explains how following his rescue of Maria Clementina which ought to have been rewarded by new positions of authority, trust and esteem in service to his king at the Jacobite court-in-exile in Rome, Sir Charles Wogan fell from James' royal favour. A discussion of court intrigue and political rivalries, the paper attempts to illuminate some of the dark corners of the Jacobite court in Rome in 1719. In later years, we are told, Wogan consoled himself with nostalgic thoughts of his ancestral home at Rathcoffey, County Kildare, to which he remained deeply attached during his exile, and with historical examples of when capable and ingenious men were undermined by lesser comrades.

In her essay on political allusions in the music dedicated to James Stuart and Maria Clementina in 1719, musicologist Aneta Markuszewska presents evocative glimpses of the pomp and ceremony attached to the young couple's marriage at Montefiascone and the general excitement generated by their presence in Rome. Drawing upon contemporary journals, diaries, letters and especially propagandist musical compositions dedicated to the newlyweds, the projection of the image of Maria Stuart as Queen in Rome is analysed. Praised for her beauty, grace, maturity, education and conversational skills in several languages, Maria Clementina apparently made a successful transition to her new status as a public figure. By all accounts, the authorities in Rome did everything in their power to ensure that she was feted officially as 'Regina di Gran Bretagna'. Organisers of the marriage chose the Carmelite nun and mystic, St Maria Maddalena de' Pazzi (1566–1607), as a fitting subject for celebrating the wedding of James

Stuart, a Catholic whose cause was supported by the Roman Curia, and Maria Clementina, also a devout Catholic. In hindsight, Markuszewska observes, the choice of this saint as the musical centrepiece of their wedding celebrations seems prophetic since Maria Maddalena, from an eminent Florentine family, at the age of 14 entered a monastery, surpassed the sisters in religious fervour and developed symptoms of anorexia and bulimia.

In the final essay, Estelle Gittins brings to light a pair of little-known Jacobite manuscripts bought by a nineteenth-century Irish tourist in Rome and now held in the Library of Trinity College Dublin – a book of devotions that belonged to the last reigning Stuart monarch, James II and the marriage certificate of his son, James III and Princess Maria Clementina Sobieska. As Gittins explains, the certificate communicated the prestige of Britain and Ireland's legitimate royal house to political supporters across Europe and is a testament to the aspirations and loyal service of thousands of Jacobites, among them the Irish hero of this story Sir Charles Wogan and his companions, who followed the Stuarts into exile and played a vital part in ensuring that the marriage took place.

Mary Ann Lyons

August 2020

ÉAMONN Ó CIARDHA

1 Irish Jacobite military exiles in Europe, 1691–1748

'The Fighting Irish': History and Memory

Sustained, widespread traffic to Europe has characterised Ireland's migration experience over 1,500 years. Close links with the Holy See and Europe's great universities, religious institutions and organisations, the English crown's extensive continental possessions and a lucrative trade in fish, wine and wool across the Irish Sea and English Channel accounts for much of this early exchange. The Reformation, Counter-Reformation and English Re-Conquest of Ireland (1534–1603) boosted this footfall; furthermore, the three wars which book-ended, bisected and defined seventeenth-century Ireland forced thousands of de-mobbed soldiers and exiled or ruined aristocrats, gentry and husbandmen into the meat-grinder of Europe's incessant, intensive confessional, dynastic and colonial conflicts. In the decades after the 'Glorious Revolution' (1688), thousands of Irish Jacobites (supporters of the exiled House of Stuart) found themselves scattered across Western Europe, where they would play a prominent role in society, including banking, the church, education, trade and, particularly soldiering.[1]

---

1   See generally, Daniel Szechi, *The Jacobites. Britain and Europe, 1688–1788*, (Manchester, 1994).

This brief reappraisal will discuss some recent developments in early modern Irish military history and historiography and explore issues of identity and ideology through the letters, life-stories, literary relics and memoirs of these exiled Irish Jacobites. It will re-examine something of their lives, social networks and links with their former patrimony, while scrutinising their political, military and cultural *milieu*, as well as their attitudes towards their exiled king and native patrimony. Furthermore, it will explore how this expatriate community remained in contact with Ireland and functioned as a military, political, diplomatic, and cultural group; how they organised recruitment networks at home and abroad and utilised Catholicism and Jacobitism for their military, political and practical advantage. Finally, it will suggest that Irish clergymen, poets, propagandists, soldiers and smugglers at once played a role in recruiting for Irish regiments in many early modern European theatres, as well as trafficking intelligence between Ireland and her exiles.

Furthermore, the Irish continental colleges, which spanned Western Europe from Iberia to the heart of Bohemia, became the early modern equivalents of embassies and consulates (or indeed Irish bars!); their clerics served as Irish regiment chaplains; they provided spiritual succour to their charges, helped them surmount cultural/language barriers, acted as notaries and witnesses for wills and testaments and looked after their widows and orphans. Recent research has also shown that Irish-born bankers, educators, lawyers and merchants often fulfilled similar roles; their careers, pan-European political, socio-economic and cultural networks tell us much about their place in their host societies.[2] After all, the early modern Irish Jacobite military formed only one part of a complex, extensive multifaceted expatriate population that organised itself in host nations from the Iberian Peninsula to the Russian Steppe. Irish banking, clerical, maritime, mercantile, political and professional communities also serviced the Irish military and their families, looking after the educational, familial, financial and spiritual welfare of their charges and facilitating contact with their native patrimony.

2   Cathaldus Giblin, ed., Catalogue of Material of Irish Interest in the Nunziatura di Fiandra', in *Collectanae Hibernica, Vols i–ix*, (1960–1968).

In this period, Irish soldiers served, staffed and led in armies from Madrid to Moscow, flitting between kingdoms, empires and republics, cultures, ideologies, languages and religions. Like other recruits, they joined for many reasons, some ideological and political, others practical and professional. Irishmen fled confessional, cultural and political persecution; others escaped famine, economic stagnation and the drudgery of a labouring life for adventure and opportunity. Family ties, regional loyalties, tradition and 'chain military migration' helped sustain this traffic. These exiles maintained strong cultural and ideological links with their native land; they marched to Irish martial music, carried the insignia of St Patrick, the Virgin Mary, the harp and red hand, and wore the red livery of the exiled Stuarts in the French and Spanish service. Furthermore, their trials, tribulations and triumphs animated their compatriots at home and throughout far-flung Irish communities. Finally, they utilised genealogy, lineage, religion and royalism to facilitate entry into (and promotion within) their chosen service; others found that these sometimes hampered or stifled a promising military or political career.

Leading luminaries and humble cannon-fodder in this service are occasionally rendered in ink, oil, marble or stone, celebrated in funeral orations, obituaries or regimental histories and remembered with various and varying degrees of enthusiasm in the history, literature and pamphlet culture of their adoptive and native countries. History, literature, journalism, art and iconography at once articulate, record and supplement its evolution, re-incarnation and transfer. Biographers, diarists and historians, Irish-language poets, Hiberno-Latin writers and Jacobite authors have both nurtured and recorded the emergence and spread of this distinct, early modern Irish nationalist identity that had loyalty to the Catholic Church and the Stuart dynasty at its core.[3] In addition to articulating, celebrating and supplementing its attendant 'Fighting Irish' cult, prickly

---

3   See Éamonn Ó Ciardha, 'Irish-language sources for the history of early modern Ireland', in Alvin Jackson, ed., *The Oxford Handbook of Irish History*, (Oxford, 2014), 439–462; Mícheál Mac Craith, 'From the Elizabethan Settlement to the Battle of the Boyne: Literature in Irish, c. 1550–1690', in Margaret Kelleher and Peter O'Leary, eds, *The Cambridge History of Irish Literature*, 2 vols, Vol. 1, (Cambridge, 2006), 74–139.

Irish writers and commentators, of whom Sir Charles Wogan is one of the most indignant and prolific, took great umbrage at both British slander and French ingratitude. By so doing, they effectively pre-empted a coterie of nineteenth-century and twentieth-century military historians, journalists and writers who lionised this venerable military tradition for their own various cultural and political ends.[4] In spite of this coverage, little is often known about the lives and experiences of the ordinary soldier who fought and died in the ranks; no over-arching study has, as yet, explored shared identities and ideologies across all the chronological and geographical expanse of Irish Jacobite military migration; nor has there been an examination of the continuities, links and shared marital traditions of the early modern and modern periods.

This 'Fighting Irish' cult, divested of its royalist, Jacobite component by middle of the nineteenth century would flavour the historical and literary writings of Young Irelanders, contemporary novelists and the leading luminaries of Irish military history.[5] Despite this, and the soldier's pivotal position in the Irish pantheon, issues of identity, ideology and popular culture, and particularly a distinct Jacobite identity, ideology and popular culture have been underplayed in recent writings on the early modern Irish diaspora and Irish military history.[6] Indeed, one could argue that the story of Irish military migration since the Nine Years War (1594–1603) is

4   John Curry (d.1780), Thomas Francis Meagher (1823–1867), John Mitchel (1815–1875), John Cornelius O'Callaghan (1805–1883), William Hartpole Lecky (1838–1903), Richard Hayes (1878–1958), William Corby (1833–1897) and the Rev James B. Sheeran CSSR (1819–1881).

5   Thomas Davis (1814–1845), Thomas Francis Meagher (1823–1867), Thomas D'Arcy Magee (1825–1868), A. M. Sullivan (1830–1884), T. D. Sullivan (1827–1914), Emily Lawless (1845–1913) Matthew O'Conor (1773–1844), J. C. O'Callaghan (1805–1883), Sir Arthur Conan-Doyle (1859–1930) and William Butler Yeats (1859–1939).

6   For example, Thomas O'Connor, *The Irish in Europe, 1580–1815*, (Dublin, 2001); Thomas O'Connor and Marian Lyons, eds, *Irish migrants in Europe after Kinsale, 1602–1820*, (Dublin, 2003); Thomas O'Connor and Marian Lyons eds, *Strangers to citizens; the Irish in Europe, 1600–1800*, (Dublin, 2008). Morley rightly points out that Irish history is still obsessed with the Protestant Ascendancy and wholly dependent on English-language sources; Vincent Morley, *The popular mind in eighteenth-century Ireland*, (Cork, 2017), 1–14.

dominated by the interlocking themes of religion, national identity and martial culture. Historians who have examined early modern Ireland's military migrants and their exploits have too often focused on buttons, badges, bugles, bayonets, battles, battalions-style regimental histories of the Irish Brigades, or on biographies of those Irishmen who rose to high political and military office.

Associational and socio-cultural aspects of the early modern, expatriate Irish military centre on a strong, distinct Irish Catholic nationalist and royalist identity, the cult of the exiled Stuarts and their native aristocracy and gentry, the cultivation of genealogy, heraldry and the centrality of their relationship to proscribed church and exiled king. Key events in the Jacobite calendar (births, birthdays, deaths and name-days) and associated rites and rituals infuse the recently digitised Stuart Papers at Windsor Castle and could provide useful chronological, methodological and thematic platforms for further research. Finally, Irish generals, colonels-proprietor and recruiters used Jacobitism to enlist kinsmen and compatriots into various European armies, often in conjunction with their diplomatic, political, propagandist and surveillance traffic on behalf of the Stuart monarch.[7]

Defeat and disillusionment at the Boyne (1690), Aughrim and Limerick (1691) initially dimmed but did not extinguish Irish enthusiasm for the Stuart cause.[8] Through the course of the late seventeenth and eighteenth centuries, often in the context of a whole series of Jacobite plots and invasion scares (1692, 1695, 1708, 1715, 1719, 1745 and 1759), Irish Jacobites looked to their exiled king, and particularly to their exiled aristocracy and gentry in the armies of France and Spain, to retrieve their confiscated lands and lost political and socio-economic and cultural status. To that end, they paid careful attention to Europe's numerous dynastic wars and colonial, military and political rivalries and their possible implications for a Stuart restoration. Thus, these commentators equated the Stuart king's return with their own repatriation, the restitution of their lands, titles and

7   Micheline Walsh, 'From Overseas archives', in *The Irish sword*, Vol. iii, (winter 1958), 268–270.

8   Breandán Ó Buachalla, *Aisling Ghéar: na Stíobhartaigh agus an t-aos léinn, 1603–1788*, (Dublin, 1996); idem, *The crown of Ireland*, (Galway, 2006), passim; Ó Ciardha, *Ireland and the Jacobite cause*, passim.

dignities, and the rehabilitation of their proscribed church; in the mean-time, they looked to their exiled monarchs for access, alms, references and titles to enable them to fully participate in the often-inaccessible world of *ancien régime* Europe.

This burgeoning Irish military diaspora, often deemed traitors, rebels and fugitives, or at best military and religious refugees in contemporary Whig writing, continued to play a significant role in European political and cultural life; moreover, they fully participated in abortive Jacobite military campaigns, invasion plots, cross-channel espionage and Irish Brigade recruitment-drives. Although the expatriate Irish military's relationship with the homeland in the seventeenth century has been the subject of much recent research, their eighteenth-century successors lack a modern, pan-European, interpretative history.[9]

'A Little Ireland in the Army of the King of France'

Approximately 19,000 Irish Jacobite soldiers left the country during and after the Jacobite wars (1689–1691), remaining a distinct military entity under King James II until respectively incorporated into the French and Spanish armies after the Treaties of Ryswick (1697) and Utrecht (1713). Arguments have raged over the exact numbers recruited for the French and Spanish service in the half-century after the Treaty of Limerick (1691). In 1729, an indignant Sir Charles Wogan lamented that over 100,000 Irishmen had died in the service of France since the 1690s; elsewhere, his letter to Dr Jonathan Swift (1667–1745), Dean of St Patrick's

---

9   Gráinne Henry, *The Irish military community in Spanish Flanders, 1586–1621*, (Dublin, 1992), passim; Robert A. Stradling, *Spanish monarchy and Irish mercenaries*, (Dublin, 1994), passim; Ó Buachalla and John McGurk also make the same point; Breandán Ó Buachalla, *Aisling Ghéar*, 432; John McGurk, '"Wild Geese": the Irish in European armies (sixteenth to eighteenth centuries)', in Patrick O'Sullivan, ed., *The Irish worldwide, identity and patterns of migration*, (London, 1992), 36.

in 1733, claimed that 120,000 had been killed in that service.[10] Writing in the early 1760s, the Abbé James MacGeoghegan (1702–1763), who dedicated his *Histoire d'Irlande* (1758) to the Franco-Irish Brigades, put the figure at 450,000 for the period between 1691 and 1745.[11] Richard Hayes, the prolific, twentieth-century Irish military historian pointed out that MacGeoghegan's figures supposed that all those who served in the Brigades were of Irish origin; Hayes himself arrived at the much more modest figure of 48,000 for the total casualties among the ranks of the Brigades in this period.[12] In more recent times, Louis Cullen put forward much smaller figures for Irish recruitment, suggesting a figure of 1,000 per annum for the 1720s and 1730s – not an insignificant number.[13]

This Irish Jacobite army, and the later Franco-Irish, Spanish-Irish regiments, provided a refuge for those who sought to overturn the revolutionary settlement, flee the Penal Laws or make military careers for themselves on the continent. Prominent Irish Catholic aristocrats and gentry and expatriate Jacobite generals and their descendants,[14] effectively retained their position at the head of this 'Little Ireland' throughout the first half of the eighteenth century.[15] Despite various military and political setbacks,

10   Éamonn Ó Ciardha, 'Jacobite Jail-breakers, Jail-birds: The Irish fugitive and prisoner in the Early Modern Period', in *Immigrants and Minorities*, Vol. 32, No. 1, (2014), 9–37.

11   Ó Ciardha, *Ireland and the Jacobite cause*, 32–33.

12   Richard Hayes, 'Irish Casualties in the French military service', in *The Irish Sword*, Vol. i, No. 3, (1949–1953), 198–201.

13   See, for example, Louis M. Cullen, 'The Irish Diaspora of the seventeenth and eighteenth centuries', in Nicholas Canny, ed., *Europeans on the move: studies in European migration*, (Oxford, 1994), 121, 124–125, 139–140; Harman Murtagh, 'Irish soldiers abroad, 1600–1800', in Tom Bartlett and Keith Jeffreys, eds, *A military history of Ireland*, (Cambridge, 1996), 294–315; Ó Buachalla, *Aisling Ghéar*, 213–214, 336–337.

14   E.g. Patrick Sarsfield, 1st earl of Lucan, d.1693; Justin MacCarthy, 1st viscount Mountcashel, d.1694; Lieutenant-General Arthur Dillon, 1670–1733; Daniel O'Brien, 4th viscount Clare, d.1693; Andrew Lee, 1650–1734; Donnogh Mc Carthy, 4th earl of Clancarthy, 1668–1734 and Colonel Gordon O'Neill, fl. 1650–1704.

15   See Nicholas Plunkett, 'A Light to the Blind', (N.L.I., MS 477, fol. 743); idem, 'Deserters of their country, the cause of its ruin' (N.L.I., MS 477, folio 9); idem,

this Irish military diaspora remained an integral part of the exiled Jacobite community. Moreover, domestic and European-based Jacobites and their political opponents on both sides of the Irish Sea considered them central to any future Stuart restoration; deeming a landing of Franco-Irish officers to be the essential catalyst for rebellion in Ireland and the latter as an important diversionary theatre in any two-pronged invasion of Southern England and the Scottish Highlands. This provided a topic of frantic correspondence between the exiled Stuart king and his supporters before successive Jacobite invasions and plots.

Recruitment

Recruitment to these Irish regiments remained the most visible manifestation of militant Jacobitism. Irishmen took shipping for the foreign service, invariably 'for the service of the Pretender', or 'James III' in surviving accounts and depositions.[16] As well as resonating with reference to invasions, plots and the machinations of prominent Jacobites on the continent, these depositions uncover extensive and intricate lines of communication between Ireland and her diaspora, via Catholic priests, Irish soldiers, Franco-Irish privateers, Irish ship-owners and merchants. Although invasion and intelligence reports survive from leading figures of the Irish

---

'To his Most Christian Majesty: the most humble petition of the Irish abroad in behalf of themselves and of their compatriots at home' (N.L.I., MS 477, p. 1); idem, 'A state of the nation' (Bodl., Carte MS 229, fol. 70); idem, 'A light to the blind' (Bodl., Carte MS 229, fols 454–455); Owen O'Malley, 'Captain Charles O'Malley to Teige, c. 1692', in Owen O'Malley, ed., 'O'Malleys between 1651–1715', in *Galway Historical and Archaeological Society Journal*, Vol. xxv, (1952), 32–46; Ó Buachalla, *Aisling Ghéar*, 188; Maurice Hennessy, *The Wild Geese*, (London, 1973), 51, quoted in Nathalie Genet-Rouffiac, 'La première generation', EPHE Doctoral Thesis, (Paris, 1995), 380, 382.

16   Breandán Ó Buachalla, 'Irish Jacobitism in official documents', in *Eighteenth-Century Ireland*, Vol. viii, (1993), 128–138; idem, *Aisling Ghéar*, 334–395; Ó Ciardha, *Ireland and the Jacobite cause*, chapters 3, 4, 5.

Jacobite hierarchy it is more difficult to glean information on the motives, opinions and sentiments of these ordinary Jacobites who took passage for foreign service in Europe.[17] However, some contemporary, albeit fragmentary accounts and these numerous recruitment depositions often shed fascinating light on the motives and activities of the ordinary foot-soldiers who took shipping to the continent in the early decades of the eighteenth century. Such depositions are replete with Jacobite political innuendo, references to impending and ongoing European wars. Recruits are assured that they would serve 'James III' and 'root out Protestants' and the process invariably concludes with a ritual drinking of the Stuart king's health. Elsewhere, recruits are promised arms, clothes and money on their arrival in France; emphasis is also placed on the covert nature of contemporary conscription.[18]

These recruiting drives are often linked to communal activity, sporting occasions (hurling/ 'commoning' and football), religious services, visits to 'holy-wells', oath-swearing and health-drinking; leading actors include farm labourers, poets, priests, publicans, the surviving Jacobite Irish aristocracy and gentry and politically suspect Protestant converts. John Brady's 1714 deposition also contain explicit data on the Irish Jacobite network, and link recruiting officers with influential continental Jacobites such as the duke of

17   See Genet-Rouffiac, 'La Première generation', 142–146, 237; Lord Fingall was in contact with St Germain via one 'Mr. White', July–August 1713; (Bodl., Carte MS 211, fols 140, 148); N.L.I., Fingall private collection, no. 6; R.A., MS 195, fol. 53; MS 212, fol. 145; 'Mémoire à la Reine d'Angleterre par le Père Ambrose O'Connor, provincial des Dominicans Irlandois', (Archives Nationalès, Fonds Guerre, MS A1 2089, fol. 182, N.L.I., MF. n. 415, p. 184) [hereafter A. N., Fonds Guerre]; Marcus de la Poer Beresford, 'Ireland in the French strategy, 1691–1789' (M.Litt., T.C.D., 1975), 53–56.

18   Information from Nantes, 16 August 1710 (N.A./P.R.O., S.P., 63/366/122); Proclamation, Shrewsbury and Council, 2 February 1714 (University Library, Cambridge, Hib.0.713.12); *Dublin Gaze*tte, 6 February 1714; 'Examination of William Lehy, Three-mile Bridge, County Waterford', 26 January 1714 (N.A./P.R.O., S.P., 63/370/219, 222); T.C.D., MS 2022, fols 105–106. One Plunkett was convicted at the assizes in Maryborough in November 1714 for trying to seduce people to serve 'James III', in John Brady, ed., *Catholics and Catholicism in the eighteenth-century press,* (Maynooth, 1965), 111, 311; Ó Buachalla, 'Irish Jacobitism in official documents', 128.

Berwick, viscount Galmoy (1652–1740) and [Lieutenant-] General [Arthur] Dillon (1670–1733).[19] Brady met a great many young Irish priests, among them one or two out of the neighbourhood of one Philip Gaffney of the parish of Currin [counties Monaghan and Fermanagh] who tried to encourage him to join the French army and anticipated a swift return to their native land.[20] He also highlighted other links between France and Ireland, identifying a priest from Cavan who communicated via London through Sir Thomas Sheridan, later one of 'the seven men of Moidart' (1684–1746) who landed with 'Bonnie Prince Charlie' at Eriskay in Scotland on 23 July 1745.[21] Finally, and crucially, there is a veritable avalanche of memoirs, invasion plots and evidence of seditious traffic.[22]

Furthermore, a relentless contemporary preoccupation with the Irish Brigades characterised Irish Jacobite literature and Whig letters; links

19   'Extract of a letter written by John Brady', Dublin, 8 February 1714 (P.R.O., S.P. 63/370/169). See also T.C.D., MS 2022, fol. 227. Brady's name is also associated with plotting in England in the 1690s; P. Melvin, 'Irish soldiers and plotters in Williamite England', in *Irish Sword*, Vol. viii, No. 52, (1979), 276. Generally, see Ó Buachalla, 'Irish Jacobitism in official documents'; idem, *Aisling Ghéar*, passim.

20   'Extract of a letter written by John Brady, dated Dublin', 8 February 1714 (N.A./ P.R.O., S.P. 63/370/169).

21   Ibid. Also see T.C.D., MS 2022, fol. 227. J. Edgar Bruns, 'The early life of Sir Thomas Sheridan (1684–1746)', in *Irish Sword*, Vol. ii, (1954–1956), 256–259. For other contemporary, seditious traffic; see 'By the grand jury of the county of Dublin', 15 June 1713 (N.A./P.R.O., S.P., 63/369/175); *Dublin Gazette*, 26–30 May 1713; (U.L., Cambs., Hib.O.713, fol. 43); (U.L., Cambs., Hib.O.714. fol. 1); Nathaniel Hooke, *The secret history of Colonel Hooke's negotiations in Scotland, in favour of the pretender, in 1707*, (London, 1760), 110, 193, 209; 'Mémoir au sujet de l'entreprise sur l'Irlande' (B.N., Fonds Français., vol. 7487, fol. 171, N.L.I., MF, 102); Marcus de la Poer Beresford, 'Ireland in the French strategy, 1691–1789' (M.Litt., T.C.D., 1975), 20–23.

22   Hooke, *Secret history*, 5, 193; 'Memoir on the means of affecting a rising in Ireland' [c.1703–1707] (B.L., Add. Ms 20, 311, fol. 68); 'Invasion plan', July 1709 (B.N., Fonds Français, 7488 fol. 228, N.L.I., mf. p. 102); Beresford 'Ireland', 20–22; A Memorial to the Marquis de Torcy', of 29 August 1710, in James Macpherson, ed., *Original papers: containing the secret history of Great Britain from the Restoration to the accession of the house of Hanover*, 2 vols, Vol. ii, (London, 1775), 165–166; 'Memoir au sujet de l'Enterprise sur l'Irlande' [c. 1706–1708] (B.N. Fonds Francais, 7487, fols 171, 173, N.L.I., MF, 102).

between the two continue to be sustained by recruitment. While contemporary recruitment depositions must be treated with caution and are subject to characteristic hyperbole and sensationalism, they do nevertheless provide intriguing, invaluable information on this proscribed trade. The majority of depositions relate to the French and Spanish service, refer to prominent international Jacobite figures and reveal intricate lines of communication between Ireland and centres of *émigré*-Irish interest, involving Franco-Irish soldiers, clerical agents, Irish ship-owners and merchants. Whig pamphleteers and politicians, for their part used the links between recruits, privateers, rapparees [outlaws] and the greater Catholic populace to claim that they intended to embark on wholesale rebellion. Finally, these depositions often have a surprisingly accurate grasp of Jacobite high-politics. Continual promises of a speedy return to Ireland with the exiled king compliment contemporary evidence of ongoing Jacobite plots and invasion plans, while affidavits placed special emphasis on commissions received directly from the Stuart claimant, the need for taking an oath to serve him and not to reveal the recruiter's identity. Recruits sought (and received) assurances that they would only serve King James and would return to receive lands and titles. Proceedings invariably concluded with a toast to the exiled king.

'The Irish Don Quixote'

As 'rebel', prisoner, fugitive, agent, diplomat, soldier and statesman, Sir Charles Wogan personified the loyalty, romance and tenacity which often characterised the Irish Jacobite *émigré* on a pan-European stage which stretched from his native Kildare, through the north of England, to France, the Papal States, the Baltic, Russia, north Africa and Spain. Col. Edward Wogan (c.1625–1654), his kinsman, had saved Charles II after the Battle of Worcester (1652), thereby copper-fastening the impeccable royalist credentials of a family that had served English monarchs in Ireland for 400 years. Sir Charles would himself add lustre to their glowing reputation by intervening spectacularly to preserve the Stuart dynasty.

Figure 1.1: Portrait of James III

Antonio David, after Martin van Meytens, *King James III*, 1725, 73.2 x 61 cm, oil on canvas (Pininski
Foundation, Liechtenstein). This portrait, like the companion portrait of Queen Clementina (on the front
cover), was painted in 1725 shortly after the birth of Prince Henry, and before Queen Clementina left the
court. The original is missing, but it was copied several times by an English painter named E. Gill who had
previously been employed in Rome by Lord Richard Howard. Gill's copies were not good, but fortunately
Antonio David was commissioned to make this one in 1730.

Wogan was heavily involved in the planning and launching of the
Jacobite insurrection against King George I in northern England in 1715.
After its failure and his capture he escaped Newgate gaol in London and
returned to James III's service in France where he again proved himself to
be a dynamic and useful servant. He formed part of a diplomatic mission
with the 2nd duke of Ormond to forge an alliance between Peter the Great
and his old foe King Charles XII of Sweden, a prelude to a proposed Jacobite

assault on their common enemy King George I.[23] An additional objective
was to identify a suitable bride for their as yet unmarried master.[24] After
successfully negotiating the marriage match between James III and Princess
Clementina Sobieska a year later, Wogan defied contemporary logistics
and the atrocious weather conditions of the Brenner Pass to snatch the
heavily guarded princess from under the noses of the imperial authorities
after she had been confined at Innsbruck.[25] He returned with Clementina
to Rome to a hero's welcome and received honours from both James and
Pope Clement XI.[26] He then entered the service of Philip V of Spain as a
military officer. His audacious rescue confounded Europe and delighted
his Jacobite contemporaries, thereby sustaining both the Jacobite cause
and enhancing the illustrious reputation of the fighting Irishman abroad.

Over the course of a long, illustrious career, Wogan never wavered in
his loyalty to the cause. He regularly corresponded with his exiled king
and retained an insatiable appetite for Jacobite plotting. Philip V of Spain
later rewarded him with the governorship of La Mancha, an appropriate
accolade for one of the most famous knights in Europe. Regular Jacobite
plots provided Wogan and other Irish Jacobites such as Lord Orrery, George
Kelly, Dennis Kelly, Edmund Bingley, John Plunkett, Francis Glascock,
Philip Neynoe, Robert Dillon, Daniel O'Carroll and a host of soldiers,
spies, fugitives, double-agents, recruiters with ample scope for intrigue.

Wogan's observations to the exiled Stuart king on the possibility of
an Irish invasion in 1729 re-emphasised the political motivation of the ex-
patriate Irish military establishment and supported the commonly held
Irish Jacobite belief that salvation would only come across the sea. Like other
Jacobite exiles (Gordon O'Neill, Arthur Dillon, Ambrose O'Callaghan,
Sylvester Lloyd and Lord Orrery) Wogan assessed the enemy's numerical

---

23   Niall MacKenzie, *Charles XII of Sweden and the Jacobites*, (London, 2002), 52. See
      also Rebecca Wills, *The Jacobites and Russia, 1715–50*, 57.
24   One possible candidate was Anna, duchess of Courland, later Tsarina Anna of
      Russia (1693–1740); however, Russia had had its share of pretenders and false
      Dimitris, Ivans and Peters.
25   See chapter 3.
26   For further discussion of Wogan's activities during this period, see chapter 4.

strength in Ireland and advocated sending a Franco-Irish expeditionary force, furnished with extra arms and accoutrements, to raise rebellion in Ireland and prevent troops from being sent from Ireland to counter the main attack on England.[27] It is significant that he based his musings on the information received from Irish *émigrés* recently returned from Ireland.[28]

Figure 1.2: Portrait of Sir Charles Wogan

Circle of Garret Morphy, *Portrait of a gentleman [Charles Wogan]*, c.1700–1710, 74 x 61cm, oil on canvas. Photo © National Gallery of Ireland. This is the only known portrait of Sir Charles Wogan. In her book *A Wife for the Pretender* (1965), Peggy Miller included an image titled 'Sir Charles Wogan as a young man' the credit for which reads '*Artist Unknown. By courtesy of Miss Agnes Tyrrell*'. It has not been possible to locate the portrait thus far.

Wogan's preoccupation with his native land also remained a recurring theme in his regular correspondence with his exiled king; moreover, he

27   Wogan to James III, 10 May 1729, (R.A., MS 127, fol. 152).
28   Ibid.

vented his considerable spleen against France for 'ill-placed and ill-timed friendship' with England and lamented 'the graves of one hundred thousand of our countrymen who died bravely without having been of any use in the cause that banished themselves' and their huge commitment in the service of a king who had ultimately betrayed their cause.[29] Similarly, Henry O'Neill l (1676–1745), the last undisputed chief of the Fews (County Armagh), who later died at Fontenoy (1745), gave precise expression to Jacobite sentiment among the Irish exiles. He highlighted his sufferings and those of his countrymen 'that have sacrificed all for the royal cause', and let King James know that 'there were some of them still in a condition to serve him after an exile of forty years'. He deemed himself to be one 'of the number and the head of a family that had the good luck to render the king, his father of blessed memory, considerable service during the late wars in Ireland' and offered him 'with zeal what I have learned during forty years in a foreign prince's service'.[30] In 1729, the ever dependable Wogan again highlighted Irish resilience, their willingness to avail of any opportunity to throw off their tyrants and the iron grip that the Catholic clergy exerted on their conscience.[31] Moreover, he suggested that recent recruiting privileges granted by Britain to the French Army in Ireland could be used to gauge militant Jacobitism, proposing that officers related to the local gentry should be sent with French passports and commissions.[32]

'The Irish Don Quixote' is probably best remembered in Irish history and letters for his voluminous correspondence with Dr Jonathan Swift (1667–1745), Dean of St. Patrick's and author of *Gulliver's Travels* (1726). After the publication of Swift's *A Modest Proposal for Preventing the Children of Poor People from Being a Burden to Their Parents or Country, and for Making Them Beneficial to the Publick* (1729), Wogan sent Swift

29　Ibid. See also (R.A., MS 112, fol. 102); Joseph Flood, *The life of the Chevalier Wogan*, (Dublin, 1922), 135–136, 141–142.

30　Henry O'Neill to Dr Cosen, 29 June 1731 (R.A., MS 146, fol. 108). See also (R.A., MS 130, fol. 167); (R.A., MS 146, fol. 107); (R.A., MS 188, fol. 197); (R.A., MS 191, fol. 20); (R.A., MS 200, fol. 112); Patrick Fagan, ed., *Ireland in the Stuart Papers*, 2 vols, Vol. i, 314.

31　Wogan to James III, 10 May 1729 (R.A., MS 127, fol. 152).

32　Ibid.

samples of his English and Latin prose, and enquired as to the feasibility of having them published in Dublin.[33] Swift reciprocated with editions of English authors, including Alexander Pope (1688–1744), Thomas Gray (1716–1771) and Edward Young (1683–1765). In subsequent missives to 'Mentor', Wogan railed at English injustices and French ingratitude. This correspondence sheds light on his patriotic *émigré mentalité* and resonates with pride at the achievements of Irishmen abroad; however, it is tempered by his graphic description of the sufferings of the Irish at home and the ingratitude of European states for their sterling service:

> Those [Irish] who have chosen a voluntary exile, to get rid of oppression, have given themselves up, with great gaiety of spirit, to the slaughter, in foreign and ungrateful service, to the number of above 120,000 men, within these forty years. The rest, who have been content to stay at home, are reduced to the wretched condition of the Spartan helots. They are under a double slavery. They serve their inhuman lordlings who are the more severe upon them, because they dare not look upon the country as their own; while all together are under the supercilious dominion and jealously of another overruling power. To return to our exiles. Mentor certainly does them that justice which cannot be denied them by any of those nations among whom they have served; but it is seldom or ever allowed them by those who can write or speak English correctly. They have shown a great deal of gallantry in the defence of foreign states and princes, with very little advantage to themselves, but that of being free; and without half the outward marks of distinction they deserved ... The only fruit the Irish have reaped by their valour is their extinction; and the general fame which they have lost themselves to accrue for their country. They have the honour of Ireland at heart, while those who actually possess their country were little affected with any other glory than that of England. Upon this account the Irish were parcelled by brigades among the many armies entertained by the French king ... The French never gained a victory, to which those handfuls of Irish were not known to have contributed in a singular manner; nor lost a battle, in which they did not preserve, or rather augment their reputation, by carrying off colours and standards from the victorious enemy ... The Irish for having been steady to their principals, and not as cunning knaves as the two neighbouring nations, have groaned, during the last two centuries, under all the weight of injustice, calumny

33   Wogan to Swift, 7 February 1732/3, in *The Works of the Reverend Dr Jonathan Swift, ... In Nineteen Volumes*, Vol. xix, 69–112; Swift to Sir Charles Wogan, September–October 1732, in *Works of Dr Swift, xviii*, 95–100.

and tyranny, of which there is no example, in equal circumstances, to be shewn in any history of the universe.[34]

He also expressed characteristically forthright views on Irish history and how it had been written by Englishmen, particularly the earl of Clarendon (1609–1674) and those 'mongrel' (Irish) historians from Richard Stanihurst (1547–1615) to William King, Archbishop of Dublin (1650–1729). His missive echoed Seathrún Céitinn/Geoffrey Keating (c.1596–1644), John Lynch (1599?–1677?) and the Abbé Mac Geoghegan in refuting the calumnies levelled against them. Finally, he blames endemic warfare, disunity and the proscription of Catholic schools for Ireland's inability to defend herself against her detractors:

All this calumny has been sounded into the ears of all Europe by their enemies, both foreign and domestic; and thereby gained credit, more or less, on account of not having been sufficiently controverted or refuted in time. Their constant misfortunes have given a sort of sanction to all this imposture and iniquity. They could not defend themselves in the midst of so much division at home, from so many powerful and confederated enemies. In the meantime, they were involved in too much war, or in too much misery, to be the relaters of their own story with any advantage; or found the English language as backward as the English nation and government, to do them common justice. Their enemies have spared them the labour with a vengeance. The mongrel historians of the birth of Ireland, from Stanihurst and Dr. King down to the most wretched scribbler, cannot afford them a good word in order to curry favour with England. ... In the meantime, it is impossible for an upright and good-natured spirit not to look with concern upon the inhuman slavery of the poor in Ireland. Since they have neither liberty nor schools allowed them; since their clergy, generally speaking, can have no learning but what they scramble for, through the extremities of cold and hunger, in the dirt and egotism of foreign universities; since all together are under the perpetual dread of persecution, and have no security for the enjoyment of their lives or their religion. ... In this uncouth attitude the Irishman must, in his own defence, and that of his whole country, be braver, and more nice in regard of his reputation, than it is necessary for any other man to be. All that he gets generally for his pains, is the character of having behaved

---

34 Wogan to Swift, 7 February 1732/3, in *Works of Dr J. Swift*, 70–75.

as might be expected from an Irishman; yet if there be any crime or mistake in his conduct, not only he, but his whole country, is sure to pay for it.[35]

Swift finally managed to ascertain the identity of his anonymous correspondent and urged him to seek a publisher in London; possibly with a view to keeping this high-profile, attainted Jacobite at arm's length. He also sent him two editions of his own works, one of which the chevalier immediately dispatched to the Stuart king in Rome. In what amounted to a 'treasonable' reply to Wogan's missive, Swift commented:

> Although I have no great regard for your trade, from the judgement I make of those who profess it in these kingdoms, yet I cannot but highly esteem those gentlemen of Ireland, who with all the disadvantages of being exiles and strangers, have been able to distinguish themselves by their valour and conduct in so many parts of Europe, I think above all other nations; which ought to make the English ashamed of the reproaches they cast on the ignorance, the dullness, and the want of courage, in the Irish natives; those defects, whenever they happen, arising only from the poverty and slavery they suffer from their inhuman neighbours, and the base, corrupt spirits of too many of their chief gentry ....[36]

In 1745, the redoubtable Wogan once again spear-headed Jacobite attempts to induce the Spanish court to provide the necessary funds and arms to supply the beleaguered Charles Edward in Scotland. As part of this campaign, he published his *Mémoirs sur l'enterprise d'Innsbruck* (1745), which he dedicated to Marie Leszczyńska, the Polish-born Queen of France, and a relative of the late Stuart queen. He later joined Henry, duke of York (1725–1807), King James' younger son, at Arras in the hope of repairing to Scotland.[37] As part of this campaign, he also sent King James a list of Irish officers in both Italy and Oran (a port city in

---

35   Ibid., 80–87. See also Éamonn Ó Ciardha, 'Irish-language sources for the history of early modern Ireland', in Alvin Jackson, ed., *The Oxford handbook of modern Irish history*, (Oxford, 2014), 439–462.

36   Swift to Sir Charles Wogan, September-October. 1732, in *Works of the Rev. Dr. Jonathan Swift*, Vol. xviii, 95–100.

37   Henrietta, Tayler, *Jacobite Epilogue: a further selection of letters from Jacobites among the Stuart papers at Windsor published by the gracious permission of his Majesty the King*, (London, 1941), 322.

north-west Algeria, a possession of Spain at the time) who would join the prince in Scotland. His characteristically upbeat letter to King James re-iterated his exile sentiments and his hopes for the restoration of his king and a return to his native land.[38] Revelling in Charles Edward's success in Scotland, he minded his stoical monarch of the prospect of a restor-ation to their respective birthrights 'and the satisfaction of seeing each other at home after so tedious and irksome a banishment'.[39] However, the optimistic Wogan would experience the agonised frustration of many Irish Jacobites in both France and Spain at the apparent unwillingness of the Bourbon kings Louis XV and Philip V to fully support the 'Forty-Five'; his disdain for French duplicity echoed his criticisms to Swift in the 1730s.

At this time, Sir Felix O'Neill (c.1720–1792) of the Fews, County Armagh, later instrumental in Charles Edward's flight to Skye and im-mortalised in verse by the Ulster poet Art Mac Cumhaigh (c.1715–1773), declared a willingness to sacrifice himself in imitation of his ancestors; he emphasised his potential usefulness in Ireland.[40] Owen O'Sullivan, an-other of the Wild Geese, wished that he had wings to follow his prince.[41] However, hard currency provided the main reason why many of these loyal, Spanish-based Irish Jacobites failed to assemble under the unfurled Stuart standard at Glenfinnan:

> You remark very well the difficulty for many of them to quit at present the em-ployments they are in, but the other reason you hint one still stronger, besides very few of them are in a condition to make that journey if the court of Spain does not order a supply for them at the same time if it grants leave for absenting themselves, and even then 'tis not everyone who would be willing to go should he be sent.[42]

38   Wogan to James III, 5 July 1745, (R.A., MS 269, fol. 49).
39   Wogan to James III, 5 October 1745 (R.A., MS 269, fol. 49).
40   Felix O' Neill to James Edgar, 26 August 1745 (R.A., MS 267, fol. 67). See also (R.A., MS 267, fol. 166; MS 267, fol. 67; MS 279, fol. 72; MS 286, fol. 169); *Ascanius or the young adventurer. A true story*, (London, 1747), 106–116. See Tomás Ó Fiaich, 'The O'Neills of the Fews', in *Seanchas Ardmhacha*, Vol. vii, (1973), 1–65; Vol. vii, (1974), 263–315; Vol. viii, (1977), 386–413.
41   Owen O'Sullivan to James Edgar, 27 August 1745, (R.A., MS 267, fol. 69).
42   William Lacy to Edgar, 2 September 1745, (R.A., MS 267, fol. 111).

The prince's exploits in Scotland animated the Irish exiles, strengthening their belief that the European political situation augured well for his affairs.[43] Having commended Charles Edward for his heroic endeavours to deliver 'His Majesty's [King James'] subjects from tyranny and usurpation', an un-named member of the O'Hanlon family alluded to the Irish exiles' hidden agenda. Attached to the French army 'whom we have followed in some expeditions', he informed James Edgar, King James' secretary that they were 'ever seeking a proper opportunity to push into Great Britain and join His Majesty's forces'.[44] Dominic Heguerty, a leading Paris-based Freemason and Jacobite agent, also promoted a Spanish-sponsored invasion of Ireland. He conferred with senior members of the French ministry including Le Comte de Maurepas, Le Comte D'Argenson and Orry, who desired that 'he would give them thoughts on the manner of conveying three Brigades to England'. Heguerty assured James 'that Your Majesty may depend on a considerable diversion in Ireland on the Spanish side'.[45]

As late as the 1750s, influential French-based Irish Jacobites, such as Myles MacDonnell and General Charles Edward Rothe (fl. 1733–1766), the illustrious veteran of the Irish Brigades, remained confident of an improvement in Jacobite fortunes.[46] Similarly, Thomas Arthur Lally, Governor of Bologna (1709–1766), whose military prowess had been proven on the fields of Dettingen (1743) and Fontenoy (1745) and at the walls of Bergen-op-Zoom (1746), believed that Charles Edward remained a powerful trump-card for France. He advocated sending a diversionary force of 8–10, 000 men to Ireland or Scotland and shared Charles Edward's optimism that

43   See J. McDonnell to James Edgar, 30 September 1745 (R.A., MS 267, fols 101).
     See also (R.A., 267, fols 150, 156; MS 268, fol. 72). See Frank McLynn, *France and
     Jacobite rising of 1745*, 81.
44   O'Hanlon to Edgar, 8 September 1745, (R.A., MS 267, fol. 157). See also (R.A., MS
     267, fol. 183).
45   Dominic Heguerty to James III, 14 September 1745 (R.A., MS 268, fol. 17); Frank
     McLynn, *France and Jacobite rising of 1745*, 55, 67, 76, 82, 176, 186–196, 214; idem,
     'Ireland and the Jacobite rising of 1745', in *Irish Sword*, Vol. xiii, (1977–1979),
     345–347.
46   Myles McDonnell to [Edgar], Corunna, 27 December 1755 (R.A., MS 360, fol.
     100). See also R.A., MS 360, fol. 162; Beresford, 'Ireland', 197.

King George II's ailing condition and the weakness of Frederick, Prince of Wales (1707–1751), George's heir, augured well for the Jacobite cause.[47] Similarly, with the outbreak of the Seven Years' War (1754–1763), prominent Irish exiles expressed confidence in the success of a French landing in Britain and again advocated a diversionary expedition to Ireland. However, the decline of the Irish interest in French military and political life, the death of influential Jacobites such as Lord Clare (d.1761) and Thomas Arthur Lally, the decline and death of James III (1766) and the subsequent descent of his son into alcoholism, scandal and 'apostasy', severed the links between the Stuart king and the Irish Brigades.[48]

Conclusion

Jacobitism provided the Irish diaspora with a meta-narrative through which they interpreted their own exile and the persecution of their Ireland-based peers. Moreover, their surviving historical and literary relics provide a fascinating insight into the complex, interconnected struggles between Irish Catholicism and Protestantism, Hanoverian and Stuart royalism and Franco-British imperialism. The activities of these Irish Jacobite exiles in the realms of diplomacy, espionage, politics and especially warfare provide a fitting testimony to their cultural fluidity, mobility and vulnerability. Their often fraught, diplomatic, military and political travails shed valuable light on the vagaries of exile, and the need to balance loyalty to the Stuarts with political and military duty to the Bourbons and Habsburgs. Their correspondence, memoirs and musings reveal a vibrant political ideology and culture that ebbed and flowed with the vicissitudes of Irish, British and European politics. Moreover,

---

47 Thomas Arthur Lally to Prince Charles Edward, 18 May 1756 (R.A 362, fol. 146); Beresford, 'Ireland in the French Strategy', 192; Hayes, *Irish swordsmen in France*, 223–247; Ruvigny, Marquis de, *Jacobite Peerage*, (Edinburgh, 1904), 119–120.

48 William Griffin, *The Irish on the continent in the eighteenth century*, (Wisconsin, 1979), 465.

they show how they themselves flourished or floundered in early modern Europe, how they interpreted their own exile and the persecution of their Ireland-based, Jacobite peers and how they viewed Ireland's role in Jacobite and European geopolitics.

Recruitment to the Irish regiments provided the crucial, tangible link between the two sections of the Irish political nation; thus, it is no surprise that the Whig authorities habitually fingered key members of the surviving Irish Catholic aristocracy and gentry, prominent Protestant converts, un-registered Catholic priests, smugglers and privateers for their involvement therein. Recruitment reports, invariably for the service of 'the Pretender' or 'James III', highlight commissions received for the Stuart king and the promise the prospective recruits that they would only serve his cause. They contain precise information on impending Jacobite invasions and vivid detail on important Jacobite exiles.

In addition to their clandestine role in recruitment, Catholic clergymen come Jacobite agents trafficked between Ireland and her exiles. Furthermore, soldiers remained in regular contact with the expatriate clerical brethren of their native diocese, they contributed to their upkeep, entrusted them with the care of their widows and children and provided for the education of the impoverished clergy of their own families, native parishes, baronies or diocese. In return, the colleges took care of the spiritual needs of their secular brethren, supplied chaplains to the Brigades and acted as useful ports of call for the newly arrived, un-initiated Irish.

This expatriate Irish Jacobite military community left an indelible mark on the politics, political culture, literature and history of eighteenth-century Ireland and Europe. In conjunction with their service to temporal and spiritual masters on the continent, they retained a strong, sentimental allegiance to their native land; links which influenced the elaboration, maintenance and survival of Jacobite ideology. During wars and invasion plots, the exiles vigorously lobbied for, with and on behalf of the exiled Stuarts; in periods of political inactivity, they commented on European politics, sought pensions, titles, preferment and continually dwelt on their exile and the persecution of the indigenous Irish. The Stuart king reciprocated this contact with the Irish military *émigrés* by repeatedly turning to Irish generals, colonel-proprietors, priests and religious to obtain favour for his loyal subjects. *Émigré* rhetoric bristled with Irish Jacobite self-righteousness and their persecution mentality. They boasted their willingness to serve the cause and return to their native lands and possessions. These declarations should not be dismissed as hollow rhetoric because many of the most influential Irish exiles kept themselves informed on the strength of the Whig garrison and they regularly and forcefully advocated an invasion of Ireland during the first half of the eighteenth century.

Bibliography

Primary Sources

Archives Nationale de France, Fonds Guerre, MS A1 2089, fol. 182, N.L.I., MF. p. 184.

Bibliothèque Nationale de France, Fonds Français., vol. 7487, fol. 171, N.L.I., MF, 102; Fonds Français, 7488 fol. 228, N.L.I., mf. p. 102.

Bodleian Library, Carte MS 229, fols 70, 454–5; MS 211, fols 140, 148.

National Archives, Public Records Office, State Papers, 63/366/122; 63/369/175; 63/370/169; 63/370/219, 222.

National Library of Ireland MS 477, fol. 743; MS 477, folio 9; MS 477, p. 1; Fingall private collection, no. 6.

Royal Archives, Windsor, MS 195, fol. 53; MS 212, fol. 145; MS 127, fol. 152; MS 112, fol. 102; MS 146, fol. 108; MS 130, fol. 167; MS 146, fol. 107; MS 188, fol. 197; MS 191, fol. 20; MS 200, fol. 112; MS 127, fol. 152; MS 269, fol. 49; MS 267, fol. 67; MS 267, fol. 166; MS 267, fol. 67; MS 279, fol. 72; MS 286, fol. 169; MS 267, fol. 69.

Trinity College Dublin, MS 2022, fols 105–6, MS 2022, fol. 227.

University Library, Cambridge, Hib.O.713, fol. 43; Hib.O.714. fol. 1.

Secondary Sources

Ascanius or the young adventurer. A true story, (London, 1747).

Brady, John, ed., *Catholics and Catholicism in the eighteenth-century press*, (Maynooth, 1965).

Cullen, Louis M., 'The Irish Diaspora of the seventeenth and eighteenth centuries',
     in Nicholas Canny, ed., *Europeans on the move: studies in European migration*,
     (Oxford, 1994).
de la Poer Beresford, Marcus, 'Ireland in the French strategy, 1691–1789', (M-Litt.
     TCD, 1975).
Flood, Joseph, *The life of the Chevalier Wogan*, (Dublin, 1922).
Genet-Rouffiac, Nathalie, 'La première generation', École Pratique des Hautes
     Études Doctoral Thesis, (Paris, 1995).
Giblin, Cathaldus, ed., Catalogue of material of Irish Interest in the Nunziatura di
     Fiandra', *Collectanae Hibernica i-ix*, (1960–1968).
Gilbert, John T., ed., *Narrative of the detention, liberation and marriage of Maria
     Clementina Stuart*, repr. (Dublin, 1984).
Griffin, William, *Irish on the continent in the eighteenth century*, (Wisconsin, 1979).
Hayes, Richard, 'Irish casualties in the French military service', in *The Irish Sword*,
     I, No. 3, (1949–1953).
Hayes, Richard, *Irish swordsmen in France*, (Dublin, 1934).
Hennessy, Maurice, *The Wild Geese*, (London, 1973).
Henry, Gráinne, *The Irish military community in Spanish Flanders, 1586–1621*,
     (Dublin, 1992).
Hooke, Nathaniel, *The secret history of Colonel Hooke's Negotiations in Scotland, in
     favour of the Pretender, in 1707*, (London, 1760).
Hughes, Lindsey, *Russia in the age of Peter the Great*, (New Haven, 1998).
Jackson, Alvin, ed., *The Oxford handbook of modern Irish history*, (Oxford, 2014).
Mac Craith, Mícheál, 'From the Elizabethan settlement to the Battle of the
     Boyne: literature in Irish, c. 1550–1690', in Margaret Kelleher and Peter
     O'Leary, eds, *The Cambridge History of Irish Literature*, 2 vols, Vol. i,
     (Cambridge, 2006), 74–139.
MacKenzie, Niall, *Charles XII of Sweden and the Jacobites*, (London, 2002).
Macpherson, James, ed., *Original papers: containing the secret history of Great
     Britain from the Restoration to the accession of the house of Hanover*, 2 vols,
     (London, 1775).
McGurk, John, ' "Wild Geese": the Irish in European armies (sixteenth to eight-
     eenth centuries)', in O'Sullivan, Patrick, ed., *The Irish worldwide, identity and
     patterns of migration*, (London, 1992).
McLynn, Frank, *Charles Edward Stuart: a tragedy in many acts*, repr. (Oxford, 1991).
McLynn, Frank, *France and Jacobite rising of 1745*, (Oxford, 1981).
McLynn, Frank, 'Ireland and the Jacobite rising of 1745', in *Irish Sword*, Vol. xiii,
     (1977–1979).
Murtagh, Harman, 'Irish soldiers abroad, 1600–1800', in Tom Bartlett and Keith
     Jeffreys, eds, *A military history of Ireland*, (Cambridge, 1996).

Ó Buachalla, Breandán, *Aisling Ghéar: na Stíobhartaigh agus an t-Aos léinn, 1603–1788*, (Dublin, 1996).

Ó Buachalla, Breandán, 'Irish Jacobitism in official documents', in *Eighteenth-Century Ireland, viii* (1993).

Ó Ciardha, Éamonn, *Ireland and the Jacobite Cause: a fatal attachment*, (Dublin, 2002).

Ó Ciardha, Éamonn, 'Irish-language sources for the history of early modern Ireland', in Alvin Jackson, ed., *The Oxford handbook of Irish history*, (Oxford, 2014).

Ó Ciardha, Éamonn, 'Jacobite Jail-breakers, Jail-birds: The Irish fugitive and prisoner in the Early Modern Period', in *Immigrants and minorities*, (London, 2013).

Ó Fiaich, Tomás, 'The O'Neills of the Fews', in *Seanchas Ardmhacha*, Vol. vii, (1973), Vol. vii, (1974), Vol. viii, (1977).

O'Malley, Owen, ed., 'O'Malleys between 1651–1715', in *Galway Historical and Archaeological Society Journal*, Vol. xxv, (1952).

Ruvigny, Marquis de, *Jacobite Peerage* (Edinburgh, 1904).

Swift, Jonathan, *The works of the Reverend Dr Jonathan Swift,... In nineteen volumes*, (London, 1765).

Szechi, Daniel, *The Jacobites. Britain and Europe, 1688–1788*, (Manchester, 1994).

Tayler, Henrietta, *Jacobite Epilogue: a further selection of letters from Jacobites among the Stuart papers at Windsor published by the gracious permission of his Majesty the King*, (London, 1941).

Walsh, Micheline, 'From overseas archives', in *The Irish Sword*, Vol. iii, (winter 1958), 268–270.

Wills, Rebecca, *The Jacobites and Russia, 1715–50*, (East Lothian, 2002).

JAROSŁAW PIETRZAK

2 The Sobieskis: *A Polish royal family in the history of Europe*

*

The genealogical legend of the Sobieski family, developed in the seventeenth and early eighteenth centuries during the reign of Jan III Sobieski, claimed that the progenitor of the family was Lestek, so-called *the Goldsmith*, who led the Lechites against the Macedonian army of Alexander the Great.[1] Lestek, guided by cunning and intelligence, made golden shields, which were positioned by him and his soldiers in such a way so that they reflected the sun's rays, which in turn blinded the enemy. For his deed and bravery, a simple craftsman was rewarded with the royal crown. Other versions claimed that the mythical creator of the Sobieski dynasty was a knight, 'Janik', fighting in the ranks of Prince Leszek called 'the Black' against the Yajvings. During the fight, Janik lost his weapon and was exposed to the enemy's attack. St Michał Archangel came to Janik's rescue. The voivode (prince) of the heavenly hosts gave him his shield, thanks to which not only did he save his life, but also the prince's. In exchange for being of help to the prince, Janik received the coat of arms and the hand of Prince Leszek's niece, thereby becoming related to the Piast dynasty. Wojciech Stanisław Chrościński, the chief literary celebrant of the deeds of Jan III Sobieski, went even further, creating an

---

1 Jarosław Pietrzak, 'Genealogical and heraldic legend Sobieski family as a part of ancestral propaganda', in *Rocznik Polskiego Towarzystwa Heraldycznego*, Vol. 25, (2016), 53–70.

imaginary picture of the unions linking the legendary ancestors of King Sobieski with representatives of foreign ruling houses. Published in 1717, this was undoubtedly an expression of aspiration of the already deceased Jan III. A ruler from the nobility, chosen by nobles, to link his family with European monarchs, to whom the crown was passed through inherited succession.[2] This essay will examine the rise to prominence of the Sobieskis through military prowess and advantageous marriage alliances from their late medieval origins to the end of their noble lineage in the eighteenth century.

The beginnings of the Sobieski family were in fact less dramatic than it was described in legend. The first member of the family entitled 'de Sobieszyn', as confirmed by source, was Mikołaj (Nicholas) the heir on Radoryż, Ulęż and Lend in Sandomierskie Voievodship. He died about 1480 and was mentioned in the 'Liber Beneficiorum' of the diocese of Cracow (Krakow) by Jan Długosz. Later, the Sobieski family moved to the Lubelskie Voievodship. Five children were born to Mikołaj (Nicholas) and Małgorzata (Margaret) Krzynicka: Sebastian, Mikołaj (Nicholas), Valentin, Zbigniew and Ursula. Sebastian Sobieski, who lived in the years 1486–1557, initiated the royal line of the family. The other brothers gave birth to the noble branches of the family. In 1516 Sebastian (I) married Barbara Gielczewska. The sons of Sebastian I were: Mikołaj (Nicholas), who died heirless in 1539; Stanislaw (I), the husband of Katarzyna (Catharine) Olesnicka; and Jan, the husband of Katarzyna (Catharine) Gdeszynska. The key figure here is Jan Sobieski, who started his military career on campaign in Ruthenia. In 1537, he was promoted to the standard-bearing cavalry unit of Stanislaw Myszkowski, Voivode of Cracow. He conducted numerous expeditions against the Tatars in 1539 and 1542. The campaign in 1542 was one of most spectacular, when Sobieski attacked the Crimean Tatar strongholds of Oczakov and Balaklava. He devoted the rest of his life, from 1552 to around 1566, to military engagements in Moldova. Importantly, together with his brother Stanislaw and father Sebastian, he participated in the

2   Anna Czarniecka, 'Nikt nie słucha mnie za życia ... Jan III Sobieski w walce z opozycyjną propagandą', (1684–1696) ['*Nobody listens to me during my lifetime ... Jan III Sobieski in the fight against opposition propaganda (1684–1696)*'], (Warsaw 2009).

Calvinist synod in Bychawa in 1560, which means that the Sobieski family was one of the followers of the Reformed faith. Jan left three sons: Marek (Mark), Mikołaj (Nicholas) and Sebastian.[3]

Among the offspring of Jan and Katarzyna (Catherina) Gdeszynska was Marek (Mark) Sobieski. He became a royal courtier and was well known for his political and military abilities. In 1577 during the Battle of Tczew at Lake Lubieszowski he became famous for his daring courage and physical strength. His fame was cemented by the war with Moscow over Livonia. King Stefan (Stephen) Batory, in recognition of his bravery, in August 1581, gave him the title of Court Standard-Bearer. Many factors contributed to Sobieski's promotion to the political elite of the country. The first determinant was undoubtedly the close relationship with the Chancellor and the Grand Crown Hetman – Jan Zamoyski, which dates back to 1579. During the *interregnum* after the death of King Stefan in 1586, probably under the influence of Zamoyski, Sobieski supported the candidacy of Zygmunt (Sigmund) Waza, against the candidacy of Archduke Maximilian Habsburg, the brother of Emperor Rudolf II. Sobieski even commanded the charge of hussars at the Battle of Byczyna, which led to the destruction of the Archduke's troops. After the victory and solemn coronation of Zygmunt in Cracow, Marek Sobieski was the overseer of captives taken by Zamoyski – including Archduke Maximilian and his supporters – at Krasnystaw, until 1589. At the court of Zamoyski, Sobieski performed various functions including the administration of his estates and as tribunal court plenipotentiary. The continuous and direct contact between Zamoyski and Sobieski led to Sobieski being recognised not only as a noble client, but also as a political supporter and legate, an active military commander, an advisor and a friend of the chancellor. Thus, Zamoyski's support and protection ensured Marek Sobieski's promotion.[4]

---

3   Jan Wimmer, 'Military traditions of the Sobieski family', in *Śląski Kwartalnik Historyczny Sobótka* 35, Vol. 2, (1981), 149–161; M. Plewczyński, 'The military ancestors of Jan III Sobieski in the 16th century', in Janusz Wojtasik, ed., *Jan III Sobieski – wódz i polityk [Jan III Sobieski – commander and politician 1629–1696]*, (Siedlce, 1997), 10–27.

4   Długosz, *Jakub Sobieski*, (Wrocław, 1989), passim; Zofia Trawicka, *Jakub Sobieski 1591–1646. Studium z dziejów warstwy magnackiej w Polsce z czasów Wazów [Jakub*

Marek first rose to political influence at the level of the Lublin diet
(legislative assembly). He was elected three times as a deputy in 1592, 1593
and 1596. Undoubtedly, the patronage of Jan Zamoyski influenced Marek's
career. In 1596 Marek was granted the office of castellan of Lublin and a
year later he was nominated to the Lublin voivode (principality). Marek's
strategic marriage alliances and family affinities opened the road leading
to the upper echelons of elite status for the Sobieski family. His first wife,
Jadwiga (Hedwig) Snopkowska, daughter of the Przemyśl castellan Stefan
(Stephen) Snopkowski, ensured her husband valuable connections with
powerful families – Herburt, Fredro and Firlej. His second wife, Katarzyna
(Catherina) Teczynska, whom he married in about 1600, belonged to the
broadly branched magnate and senatorial family, boasting the title of count
earned from the Emperor in 1527. In addition to family connections with
the great princes of the Zbaraski, Olelkowicz-Słucki and Radziwiłł, she
dowered him with extensive estates in Małopolska.[5] However, Marek's
greatest financial achievement at this time entails the purchase of the title
to the lands from *Złoczów* in Red Ruthenia in 1598. Apart from *Złoczów*
(town and castle), they comprised from 40 to 60 villages. These were the
beginnings of the latifundium,[6] bringing important profits from the sale
of grain and wood to the Sobieski family. This, in turn, allowed Marek to
be politically independent. The grandfather of King Jan III, which should
be emphasised, appeared in Ruthenia as a new host, not connected with
the local nobility, which guaranteed him relative independence.[7]

The first marriage of Marek Sobieski, contrary to the second one, resulted in numerous offspring: five daughters and a son – Jakub (James),
the future father of the king. His first daughter, Zofia (Sophia), married

---

     *Sobieski 1591–1646. A study on the history of the magnate in Poland in the era of Vasa
     dynasty]*, (Kraków, 2007), passim.

5   Janusz Kurtyka, *Latyfundium Tęczyńskich. Dobra i ich właściciele [Tęczyński lati-
     fundium. Estates and owners]*, (Kraków, 1999), passim.

6   The term used to describe large privately held estates of the high nobility.

7   Magdalena Ujma, *Latyfundium Jana Sobieskiego [Latifundium of Jan Sobieski]*,
     (Opole, 2005); see also Henryk Litwin, *Napływ szlachty polskiej na ziemie
     ukrainne w latach 1569–1648 [The inflow of Polish nobility to Ukraine 1569–1648]*,
     (Warsaw, 2000).

voivode Jan Wodynski. The second, Aleksandra Marianna, was the wife of the Great Marshal of Lithuania Krzysztof (Christopher) Wiesiolowski. The third of the sisters, Katarzyna (Catherine), married the voivode of Leczyca, Stanislaw Radziejowski, and was the grandmother of the Primate – Michał Stefan Radziejowski. The next one, Gryzelda married the voivode of Dorpat Dadźbog (Deodatus) Karnkowski, and after his death the starosta (magistrate) of Odolanowo Jan Rozdrażewski. Last – Anna joined the monastery of Saint Bridget in Lublin in 1610, but died as prioress in Grodno in 1646. It seems that Sobieski was conducting a well-thought-out marriage policy, building the power of the family based on the unions of his daughters with high-born bachelors, occupying senate and dignitary offices. It was at this time that Marek Sobieski converted to Roman Catholicism due to its resilience in the region. A possible reason for his conversion could relate to his entry to the senate, where the alliance of the ruling class with the Catholic Church was established. This change was likely also influenced by the lack of a strong leadership in the reformation camp, the withering of the ideology of the movement, and related disputes in the bosom of Protestantism. Thus, Marek Sobieski became the first magnate in the family.[8]

After the death of Marek in 1605, his eldest son, Jakub, became the head of the family. Born in 1591 he became one of the most important figures on the political scene of the Polish-Lithuanian Commonwealth and completed his father's work on strengthening the position of the family as well as consolidating its position at magnate status. Preparing him for this role, his father sent him to study first at the Zamość Academy, and then at the Cracow Academy. The rest of his education was completed during a journey through Europe spanning the years 1607–1613. He spent time in the Reich (Holy Roman Empire), France, the Netherlands, England, Spain, Portugal and the Italian states. Education gained in this way allowed him to appear on the forum of the political life of his various host

---

8   Andrzej Kazimierz Banach, 'Conversions of Protestants to Catholicism in the Crown in 1560–1600', in *Seria Historica*, Vol. 77, (1985), 21–35.

countries, either in diplomatic negotiations, or as an orator at private ceremonies.[9] In October 1624, Jakub received from Zygmunt III the title of starosta (mayor) of the Trembowla, and later of Krasnystaw. In 1628, he received titular crown prowess, which had binding significance only at the royal court. These titles and offices, though certainly prestigious, in fact placed Jakub quite low in the hierarchy of officials of the Polish-Lithuanian Commonwealth, the Rzeczpospolita.[10] A more serious promotion took place during the reign of Władysław (Vladislav) IV. In 1633 Jakub was made the starosta of Jaworow, and five years later the voivod of Belz, which was associated with the senatorial rank. This distinction was bestowed, not only for the need to express gratitude for Jakub's efficient management of the parliamentary chamber, but also because Władysław IV wanted to win support from key members of the nobility. Similarly, Władysław IV's gift of the office of the voivode of Ruthenia to Jakub in 1641 can be interpreted in the same way. He was promoted in 1646 as a castellan of Cracow, the highest ranking civil senator.[11]

His foreign education, covering not only schooling, traveling and visiting interesting places, but also getting to know life and people in other countries and foreign courts, resulted in great knowledge and experience. Jakub mastered several languages including Latin, Greek, German, Italian, French and Turkish and was often invited to participate in diplomatic talks, for example, with Russia in 1618, with Turkey in 1621 and with Sweden in 1628 and 1635. Jakub was also the author of several memoirs, including 'Peregrination in Europe' (1607–1613) and 'Road to Baden' (1638), 'Diary of the Moscow expedition from 1617–1618', 'Diary of the

---

9   Jan Sobieski, *Peregrynacja po Europie (1607–1613). Droga do Baden (1638)* [*Peregrination around Europe (1607–1613) Road to Baden (1638)*], Jósef Długosz, ed., (Warsaw-Wrocław-Kraków, 1991).

10 For full discussion of the structure of power in Poland-Lithuania see Zbigniew Góralski, *Urzędy i dygnitarstwa w dawnej Rzeczypospolitej* [*Offices and dignities in old Poland*], (Warsaw, 1983).

11 Aleksandra Skrzypietz, 'Foreign "language if we need it then" – "foreign" and "our" in the eyes of Sobieski', in Filip Wolański, ed., *Staropolski ogląd świata – problem inności* [*Old Polish view of the world – the problem of otherness*] (Toruń, 2007), 162–183; Zofia Trawicka, 'The extrajudicial political activity of Jakub Sobieski', in *Śląski Kwartalnik Historyczny Sobótka*, Vol. 2, No. 35, (1980), 171–174.

Chocim expedition in 1621' and 'Diary of intercession and the coronation of Władysław (Vladislav) IV from 1633'. Sobieski's works also include numerous and erudite funeral speeches, original epitaphs and letters.[12]

During his lifetime, Jakub participated in many military expeditions, including the expedition of Prince Władysław to Moscow in 1617. Four years later, he faced the Turks at Chocim in 1621. Three years later he fought against the Tatars in defence of Trembowla and in the battle of Martynow. In 1634, he took part in an expedition against the Turks near Kamieniec, fighting against the Turkish troops of Mehmed Abaza, governor of the Ottoman province of Sylistria.

Sobieski's magnate position was consolidated by two marriages, just like in the case of his father. He entered into the first marriage in 1620 with Marianna, the Princess Wisniowiecka, daughter of the duke Konstanty Wisniowiecki and Anna of Zahorowscy. However, neither of them experienced marital happiness, because Jakub, who was involved in the military expedition against the Turks and peace mediation, was rarely home. Marianna died unexpectedly in 1624 which had a deep impact on Jakub. He struggled to come to terms with the loss and was deeply affected by her death.[13] In 1627 he remarried to Zofia Teofila (Sophia Theophila) from Danilowicze. She was granddaughter to Stanislaw Żółkiewski, the Chancellor and Grand Hetman of Crown, who in 1610 after the victory at Kłuszyn took Moscow and decades later died a hero's death at Cecora in a military engagement with the Turks in 1620.[14]

The Sobieski family attained their highest position among the elite thanks to the activity of Jakub's second son, Jan (John), who was born in 1629. His elder brother Marek (Mark) Sobieski, with whom Jan jointly

---

12 Zofia Trawicka, 'Wedding and funeral speeches by Jakub Sobieski', in Henryk Suchojad, ed., *Weddings, baptisms and funerals in the 16th–17th centuries. Culture of life and death* [*Śluby, chrzciny i pogrzeby w XVII I XVII wieku. Kultura życia i śmierci*], (Warsaw, 2001), 173–186.

13 Ilona Czamańska, *Wiśniowieccy. Monografia rodu* [*Wiśniowieccy. The monography of family*], (Poznań, 2007), 156–157.

14 Jerzy Besala, *Stanisław Żółkiewski*, (Warsaw, 1988); Aleksandra Skrzypietz, 'Teofila Sobieska née Daniłłowicz – "not a female but male heart" woman', in *Wschodni Rocznik Humanistyczny*, Vol. 2, (2005), 29–53.

received education at the Cracow Academy and then travelled abroad in 1645–1648, was killed during the battle of Batoh in 1652 with the Cossacks and Tatars.[15] Jan began his military career with skirmishes with Tatars in 1653. A year later, he was a member of the diplomatic mission of Mikołaj (Nicholas) Bieganowski to Constantinople. This contact with various peoples in the region allowed him to become proficient in Italian, French, Spanish, German, Turkish and even Tatar until the end of his life. As well as gaining valuable military experience, these formative years instilled in him scientific passions, including those related to astronomy, theology, architecture and other arts. Jan inherited the titles of starosta of Jaworow in 1644 and that of Standard-Bearer of the Crown from 1656, after he displayed especial zeal in favour of the court of King Jan II Kazimierz Vasa against the Swedes, who had invaded Poland in 1655. As the ally of the Polish king, between 1661 and 1665 Jan Sobieski supported a motion for election during the lifetime of the king (*vivente rege*), opting for Louis II Bourbon-Condé. The candidacy of the French prince was a result of secret arrangements between Marie Louise Gonzaga de Nevers, queen of Poland-Lithuania, and the French court. King Louis XIV tried to get rid of his main opponent and former participant of Fronde of the Princes (1650–1653).[16] This case led to his conflict with the Grand Marshal of the Crown, Jerzy (George) Sebastian Lubomirski. The parliamentary court, which recognised Lubomirski as a traitor because he opposed royal authority, decided to deprive him of his full office, which was then handed over by the king to Sobieski in 1665. A year later, Jan was appointed a

---

15   For the education of Marek and Jan Sobieski see Henryk Barycz, *Rzecz o studiach w Krakowie dwóch generacji Sobieskich* [*The thing about studying in Krakow of two generations of Sobieski*], (Kraków, 1984); Karolina Targosz, *Jana Sobieskiego nauki i peregrynacje* [*Jan Sobieski's education and peregrinations*], (Wrocław-Warsaw, 1985).

16   Mirosław Nagielski, *The Franco-Austrian rivalry in the Polish-Lithuanian Commonwealth during the late reign of Jan Kazimierz Waza*, in Ryszard Skowron, ed., *Poland in the face of great conflicts in modern Europe. On the history of diplomacy and international relations in the 15th-18th centuries* [*Polska w obliczu wielkich kofliktów w nowożytnej Europie. Studia z historii dyplomacji i stosunków międzynarodowych od XV do XVIII wieku*], (Kraków, 2009), 385–406.

Field Hetman (Commander) of the Crown.[17] His military success and official promotions were enhanced by his marriage to Maria Kazimiera de la Grange d'Arquien.

Maria Kazimiera de la Grange d'Arquien was born in 1641 in Nevers, France. She belonged to an old family with connections to the French Capetian Dynasty, including the Bourbons themselves. However, the greatness of the de la Grange d'Arquien family had passed long ago. Maria's father, Henri Albert d'Arquien (1613–1701) was the son of the governor of Calais and first the captain, then the colonel of the regiment of Gaston under the Duke of Orléans. In 1651 he was appointed Field Marshal of the French Army and three years later the commander of the Swiss Guard. In turn, the mother to the future queen was Françoise de la Châtre, sister of Marie Louise Gonzaga's governess. Marie arrived in Poland with her attendant in 1646, however as a result of internal unrest and Marie Louise's uncertain situation after the death of Władysław (Vladislav) IV, she was sent back to France. There she was given a simple education in the Ursuline Monastery in her hometown of Nevers and under the watchful eye of her aunt, Countess de Maligny at the Prie castle.[18]

Maria Kazimiera probably returned to Poland in 1649 and became a lady-in-waiting to queen Louise Marie. Maria Kazimiera's beauty moved the hearts of numerous magnates. Finally, in 1658 she married the voivode of Sandomierz and owner of large estates, Jan 'Sobiepan' Zamoyski. Fascination and charm were quickly overtaken by regret and sadness. Maria Kazimiera's desperation was a result of her spouse's riotous lifestyle,

---

17 Witold Kłaczewski, *Jerzy Sebastian Lubomirski*, (Wrocław, 2002); Andrzej Haratym, 'Jan Sobieski as the Crown Field Hetman (May 1666–February 1667)', in Mirosław Nagielski, ed., *Old Polish martial art of the 16th–17th century*, (Warszawa, 2002), 199–237; Mirosław Nagielski, 'Jan Sobieski – difficult beginnings of the career of the Turkish conqueror near Vienna', in *Biblioteka Epoki Nowożytnej*, Vol. 2, (2015), 45–64.

18 Maciej Serwański, 'Être une reine étrangère: deux Françaises en Pologne [To be a foreign queen: two French women in Poland]', in Isabelle Poutrin and Marie-Karine Schaub, eds, *Femmes et pouvoir politique. Les princesses d'Europe XVe-XVIIIe siècle*, (Rosny-sous-Bois, 2007), 193–200; see also Kazimierz Waliszewski, *Marysieńka. Marie de la Grange d'Arquien Reine de Pologne femme de Sobieski 1641–1716*, (Paris, 1898).

including drunkenness, an inclination to wasting money and a tendency for affairs. Furthermore, the lack of offspring did not help to improve their life together. Maria Kazimiera had been infected with syphilis by her husband and as a result would lose children before they were born, and those that were born did not survive long. It was in this sorrowful moment of her life that Maria Kazimiera started corresponding with a good friend to the Zamoyski family, the Standard-bearer of the Crown and the Jaworów *starosta*, Jan Sobieski. Declaring their feelings in ever more courageous correspondence, the lovers contemplated their uncertain and foggy future considering the reactions of their relatives and the royal couple. In 1665, Astrée and Céladon, as Maria Kazimiera Zamoyska and Jan Sobieski referred to one another to mislead any potential unauthorised readers of their letters, swore that they would get married in the future. The moment occurred four years later. They were first married in secret in May 1669, only with the knowledge of the queen. Only in July of the same year, after Zamoyski's death, their relationship was blessed once more, this time officially by the Apostolic nuncio in Poland Antonio Pignatelli.[19]

During the years 1669–1674 as the wife of Marshal and Field Hetman, and later the Grand Hetman of the Crown, Maria Kazimiera devoted herself to giving birth to offspring. Numerous childbirths (as many as nine out of twelve of Sobieski's children, among them Teresa Teofila (Theresa Theophila), Adelajde Teresa (Adelaide Theresa), Maria Teresa (Marie Therese) and Jan died over the years 1669–1683 and health complications prevented her temporarily from participating in political life. The breakthrough year was the year of 1673 when, in November, king Michał (Michael) I died; but on the following day Jan III Sobieski won a spectacular victory against Hussein Pasza's army in the Battle of Chocim on 11 November. The victorious Jan, who had had numerous successes in the struggles against the Tatars, Cossacks and Turks, was nominated for consideration as the new Polish monarch. His candidacy met with mixed opinions and speculations. The Lithuanian magnates and some of the representatives of the noble opposition from the Crown, inimical to him, looked

---

19   Aleksandra Skrzypietz, ' "Great love is full of fear" – romance of Jan Sobieski and Maria Kazimiera', in *Biblioteka Epoki Nowożytnej*, Vol. 2, (2015), 29–44.

favourably at other candidates, namely the Prince of Condé and Prince Charles Alexander of Lorraine. Thus, the leaders of the Commonwealth once again found themselves in the hostile camps of two great powers – the Holy Roman Empire and the Kingdom of France, which sought to consolidate their influence in Central and East-Central Europe. It needs to be added that Sobieski himself was not sure and initially denied any rumours of his participation in the election.[20]

Maria Kazmiera, during the interregnum, showed great activity and her actions all aimed to secure the royal crown for her husband. Thanks to her contact with the ambassadors of Louis XIV in Berlin and Warsaw, she managed to raise funds to bribe the nobles who voted for the election of the monarch. With this move, she destroyed the plans of Sobieski's opponents and led to his election on 21 May 1674. During her twenty-two-year period of being queen-consort, Maria Kazimiera interfered with the activity of many power institutions, including the Sejm (consisting of three states: the king, the chamber of deputies and the senate), regional assemblies, organs of the noble self-government of the lands and provinces of the Polish-Lithuanian Commonwealth, and also the Crown Tribunal. The queen was a promoter of many endeavours, both secular and clerical. At the same time, she recommended monarchs worthy of holding the highest offices, thus forming a political court faction. Maria Kazimiera did it with the hope of providing one of three sons – Jakub (James), Aleksander or Konstanty – with the elective throne of Poland, (see Figure 2.1). Apart from her influence on domestic politics, the queen influenced the main directions of foreign policy, leading to the conclusion in 1675 of a political alliance with France, which with the support of Sweden and Turkey was a counterweight to the Habsburgs. This change of the geopolitical situation led to the territorial expansion of the Ottoman Empire into Habsburg territory which resulted in an alliance with Vienna from 1678 to 1683. The queen's continued work resulted in the signing of a non-aggression treaty between the Rzeczpospolita and the Holy Roman Empire on 1 April 1683.

---

20   Thomas M. Barker, *Double Eagle and Cresent. Vienna's Second Turkish Siege and its historical setting*, (New York, 1967), 52, 107, 115, 159; John P. Spielman, *Leopold I of Austria*, (New Brunswick-New Jersey, 1977), 111; see also Zbigniew Wójcik, *Jan Sobieski, king of Poland*, (Warsaw, 1983).

A few months later on 12 September King Jan III won his most famous victory at the relief of the Siege of Vienna, taking the Turkish camp in the rear at the head of his famous Winged Polish Hussars.

Figure 2.1: Queen Maria Kazimiera with her son Jakub

Unspecified painter from court circle of Jan III Sobieski, *Portrait of Queen Maria Kazimiera with her son Jakub*, c1676, 107 x 85cm, oil on canvas. Courtesy of Museum of Nieborów and Arkadia, a branch of the National Museum of Poland in Warsaw.

The following years, however, showed that friendship was not permanent. The joining of Jan III to the Holy League in 1684 imposed on the Polish king the obligation to fight in Wallachia and in Moldova in 1686 and 1691, and also in Kamieniec-Podolski in 1687, which his wife closely followed. During that time the helm of government was taken over by

Maria Kazimiera, as an informal 'regent', although Sobieski did not limit, cede or resign his powers. An expression of the queen's skill and competence was the negotiation of a military and trade treaty with the King of France in September 1692. The 'Crown of the North' alliance restored the relations between Paris, Copenhagen, Stockholm and Warsaw.[21] It guaranteed a French loan for the maintenance of the Bourbon party over the Vistula River and French aid in the event of the attack by the Republic of Brandenburg, Russia or the Holy Roman Empire. For the queen, the treaty carried another advantage in terms of its trade in grain and wood products on ships flying its flag between Gdansk and Dunkirk.

The queen's latter years were turbulent however. Dynastic ambitions for the Sobieskis were dashed when in 1696 King Jan III died, followed by the defeat of Prince Jakub Sobieski by the elector of Saxony, Frederic Augustus I, in 1697 in the election for the throne. Quarrelling between the sons of King Jan III over the inheritance of his properties ensued. Furthermore, the unfavourable opinion of the nobility towards the queen-widow forced Maria Kazimiera to flee to Rome under the pretext of a pilgrimage to the Eternal City on the occasion of the jubilee year. She stayed in Rome from 1699 to 1714.[22] Her time there appears to have been fraught with further distress and unhappiness. Between her father's death in 1708 and numerous misunderstandings with Pope Clement XI as a result of her will to influence European affairs, the queen requested Louis XIV's permission to return to

---

21   Janine Fayard, *Attempts to build a 'Third Party' in North Germany 1690–1694*, Ragnhild Hatton, ed., *Louis XIV and Europe*, (Plymouth, 1976), 213–240; Aleksandra Skrzypietz, ' "Regent" of Poland – facts and myths in the biography of Maria Kazimiera', in Bożena Czwojdrak and Agata A. Kluczek, eds, *Kobiety i władza w czasach dawnych* [*Women and power in ancient times*], (Katowice, 2015), 380–393.

22   The following are excellent sources for Maria Kazimiera: *I Sobieski a Roma. La famiglia reale polacca nella Città Eterna*, Juliusz A. Chrościcki, Zuzanna Flisowska, Paweł Migasiewicz, eds, (Warsaw, 2018); Gaetano Platania, *Gli ultimi Sobieski e Roma. Fasti e miserie di una famiglia reale polacca tra Sei e Settecento (1699–1715)*, (Rome, 1989); Aneta Markuszewska, *Festa i muzyka na dworze Marii Kazimiery Sobieskiej w Rzymie (1699–1714)* [*Festa and music at the court of Maria Kazimiera Sobieska in Rome (1699–1714)*], (Warsaw, 2012); Komaszyński, *Marie Casimire*, (Katowice, 1995).

France. After a two-year residence in Blois, the Polish queen-widow died on 17 January 1716.

***

Part of Maria Kazimiera's international policies and negotiations were the marriages of her children. Along with international treaties, they were to provide a royal crown to one of the Sobieskis. Great importance was attached to the dowry of the future wife, from whom it would be possible to pay the nobility in exchange for her votes and to secure broad and strong political influence. Let us note, that in Rzeczpospolita, unlike in other parts of Europe where the law of succession to the throne prevailed, the fate of royal children, their education, the issue of giving them goods and their marriages were not private matters of the royal family. In essence, these were issues closely related to internal and foreign policy and, for this reason, dependent on the will of the nobility which met at the national assembly, the *Sejm* (Diet).

Great importance was attached to finding the right candidate for a wife for the eldest son – Jakub Sobieski. Around 1680, the king planned to give his first-born to Ludwika Karolina (Louise Charlotte) née Radziwiłł, the daughter of the Lithuanian magnate Bogusław Radziwiłł and the sole heir to his vast estates in the Grand Duchy of Lithuania. Meanwhile, without the consent of King Jan III, Ludwika Karolina gave the Margrave of Brandenburg, Louis Hohenzollern, her hand in marriage. Eventually, the case was brought to the Sejm in Warsaw in January 1681. When the news reached the capital about the marriage by Ludwika Karolina, Jan III gave his consent under the condition of payment of 40,000 thalers and an oath that Margrave Louis would not in the future become the opponent of Prince Jakub in his bid to obtain the Polish crown.[23]

---

23   Aleksandra Skrzypietz, *Królewscy synowie – Jakub, Aleksander i Konstanty Sobiescy* [*The Royal sons – Jakub, Aleksander and Konstanty Sobieski*], (Katowice, 2011); idem, 'Prince Jakub Sobieski and his contacts with European courts after the outbreak of the Great Northern War', in *Wieki Stare i Nowe*, Vol. 4, No. 9, (2012), 20–43.

After some shifting preferences between Habsburgs and the Bourbons, Jakub was offered to marry the Archduchess Maria Antonia of Austria in 1681, and later to the sister of the Elector of Bavaria, Violante Beatrice in 1683. The strong involvement of Jan III in the activities of the Holy League against the Turks and the search for more allies in Europe led to the offer of marriage of Jakub to the Portuguese Infanta Izabella Louise in 1684; and to the niece of Louis XIV, Elizabeth Charlotte de Chartres, to be considered in 1685, in order to overcome the reluctant attitude of France. When these various calculations and offers had failed, after the sudden death in 1687 of Margrave Louis Hohenzollern the Polish court returned to the plan of Jakub's marriage to Ludwika Karolina née Radziwiłł. Jakub had the strongest position among the high-ranking opponents who included Louis of Baden (1655–1707), Charles Philip Wittelsbach prince of Pfalz-Neuburg (1661–1742) and George Louis of Hanover (1660–1724), who in 1714 assumed the thrones of Britain and Ireland as George I. Ludwika Karolina expressed her willingness to meet Jakub, which took place in Berlin in August 1688 and provided him with a written promise that she would marry him, guaranteeing the contract with all her property. Despite this, after Jakub's departure, the Hohenzollerns also entered marriage negotiations with Charles Philip Wittelsbach, thereby arousing the anger of the Polish king. As a result, the oath given to Sobieski was broken and Ludwika Karolina gave her hand and rights to vast lands in the Grand Duchy of Lithuania to the Hohenzollerns. King Jan III felt this as a deep insult. The Polish king decided to occupy Ludwika Karolina's estates in Lithuania, as a form of revenge to her embezzlement and humiliation of the crown.[24]

---

24 Tadeusz Wasilewski, *Ludwika Karolina z Radziwiłłów* in *Polski słownik biograficzny*, Vol. 18, (1980), 110–112; Aleksandra Skrzypietz, *Jakub Sobieski*, (Poznań, 2015), 146–148.

Figure 2.2: Engraving of Jan III and his Family

Benoît Farjat, after Henri Gascar, *Ioannes III Rex Poloniae Invictissimus etc. Gloria par gestis compar Virtutibus Uxor. Almula Naturum Fama, parentis erit. [Jan III Invincible King of Poland etc. His Glory matches the comparable virtues of his wife. He will be a kind natural traditional parent]*, 1693, 43.7 x 62.8 cm, 1 graph: copper (National Library of Poland, Warsaw). This is a copperplate engraving from 1693 showing (from left): Konstanty Władysław, Jakub Ludwik, depicted in the framed portrait King Jan III, Aleksander Benedykt, Queen Maria Kazimiera and Teresa Kunegunda.

The question of Jakub's marriage-matches and all the related quarrels continued until 1691. Under the agreement between the Polish king and the Holy Roman Emperor, the Polish prince was given the hand of the Emperor Leopold I's sister-in-law Jadwiga Elżbieta (Hedwig Elizabeth) Wittelsbach. As a result, the Sobieski royal house became affiliated with many European dynasts. The sisters of Jadwiga Elżbieta were Eleonor Magdalen (1655–1720) wife of Emperor Leopold I; Marie Sophie (died 1748) wife of the Portuguese King Peter II Braganza; Dorothy Sophie (died 1748) wife of Odoard II Farnese, Prince of Parma and Piacenza; Marie Anna (died 1740) wife of the Charles II of Habsburg, King of Spain. Her brothers were, in turn, Palatinate electors: Philip Wilhelm (died 1693), John Wilhelm (died 1716) and Charles Philip (died 1742); Prince-Bishop of Worms and

Archbishop-Elector of Trier, Wroclaw and Mainz, Francis Louis (died 1732) and Alexander Sigismund, Bishop of Augsburg (1663–1737).[25]

Another matrimonial success was the marriage of the daughter of Jan III – Teresa Kunegunda (Theresa Kunegundis) to the Bavarian elector Maximilian II Emanuel. The Sobieskis, deciding on the person of the Bavarian elector and governor of the Spanish Netherlands, did not want to clearly declare their sympathy for or against the emperor, but rather they reserved the possibility of freely deciding on the direction of foreign policy. Teresa's marriage was sealed with a marriage agreement in May 1694, and in August that year there was a marriage *per procura* in Warsaw. In January of the following year the new electress took her seat in Brussels and from that time began to share the joys and sorrows of her husband. In 1695, she survived the bombardment of Brussels by the French troops of Louis XIV and, with the outbreak of the War of the Spanish Succession, she was forced to leave for Munich five years later. As a regent of the Bavarian Electorate in the years 1702–1705, she guarded the territorial status of the authorities, presided over the war councils, cared for the economic condition and affluence of the subjects, and supported religious and charitable foundations. The violation of peace by Holy Roman Emperor Joseph I resulted from 1705 in Teresa Kunegunda's exile in Venice, away from her husband. The reunion of the spouses took place only in 1715 in Munich, where the electress remained until the death of her husband in 1726. She returned to Venice and died there in 1730. It is worth adding that the descendant of the electoral couple, Charles Albert Wittelsbach, during the First Silesian War in 1741 subdued the Kingdom of Bohemia and forced Marie Theresa (Queen of Bohemia and Hungary, the uncrowned Holy Roman Empress) to flee to Hungary. In January 1742, the Reich Diet chose him Holy Roman Emperor, which he held until his death in 1745.[26]

---

25 Werner Hesse, *Hier Wittelsbach, hier Pfalz. Die Geschichte der pfälzischen Wittelsbacher von 1214—1803*, (Landau/Pfalz, 1986), 179–183; Jarosław Pietrzak, 'Because of these times I see very little genuine love. Marie Casimire's relationship with female members of the Sobieski family', in Anna Kalinowska and Paweł Tyszka, eds, *Maria Kazimiera Sobieska (1641–1716). W kręgu rodziny, polityki i kultury*, (Warsaw, 2017), 51–89.

26 Michał Komaszyński, 'Die politische Rolle der bayerischen Kurfürstin Theresia Kunigunde [The political Role of the Bavaraian Elector Theresia Kunigunde',

Plans to marry the other sons of Jan III Sobieski and Maria Kazimiera
to high-ranking families did not come to pass. The second of the sons of
the royal couple, Aleksander along with the youngest brother, Konstanty,
travelled in France during the years 1694–1696, where they visited the court
of Louis XIV. During that time Maria Kazimiera, wanting to secure the
future of her younger sons, tirelessly looked around for suitable candidates
their strategic marriages. Through her correspondence, there appears to have
been an endless list of princesses Aleksander could marry. According to
Maria Kazimiera, the daughter of Duchess d'Enghien could be an excellent
candidate. The princess was 30 years old, but she had a dowry of 100,000
livres. Unfortunately, on reading the letter it is not clear to whom exactly
it relates. Perhaps Maria Kazimiera meant one of the daughters of Louis
de Bourbon-Condé. At that time, three princesses were unmarried at his
home – Louise Elisabeth born in 1693, Louise Anne born in 1695 and Marie
Anne who was somewhat younger. At one time, the queen planned a marriage of her son with the aunt of the above-mentioned Duchess d'Enghien,
only 32 years old, and therefore still held the promise of bearing children;
at another, it could be the daughter of Henry III de Bourbon-Condé. The
queen was aware that her son's bachelor status was a consequence of negli-
gence from the time when Jan III was still alive. However, she was convinced
that he would accept everything that she now tried to do for him, because
he always agreed with her opinions on the family. When Aleksander declared that the potential marriage partners should at least like each other it
caused further worry to Maria Kazimiera who complained that Konstanty
probably thought the same. She emphasised that she was doing her best to
make their father's name survive by looking for the most suitable wives, and
that her sons did not care about their unstable situation. Once more, Maria
Kazimiera tried to win for the sons one of the daughters of the deceased

in *Zeitschrift für Bayerische Landesgeschichte*, Vol. 45, (1982), 555–574; idem, 'Die
Beziehungen zwischen den Höfen der Wittelsbacher und dem von Sobieski in
der zweiten Hälfte des XVII. Jahrhunderts [Relations between the Wittelsbach
and Sobieski courts in the second half of the seventeenth century]', in *Zeitschrift
für Bayerische Landesgeschichte*, Vol. 46, (1983), 512–535; Reginald de Schryver,
'Princess Teresa Kunegunda Sobieska 1676–1730. Thirty-five years of solitude', in
Tatjana Soldatjenkova and Emmanuel Waegemans, eds, *For East is East: Liber
Amicorum Wojciech Skalmowski*, (Leuven-Paris-Dudley, 2003), 165–180.

Prince Jan Frederic von Braunschweig-Lüneburg, during Sobieski's stay at the court in Hanover in 1694, but again she was disappointed.

Both of the princes went to Rome in 1700, where together they were awarded the Order of the Holy Spirit. Soon after, in 1704, the king of Sweden, Charles XII and a group of Polish magnates, supported Aleksander's candidacy for the Polish throne. During that time the possibility of marriage between Aleksander and Princess Ulrice Eleonora was being considered. According to one of the remittances, Charles XII had to submit to such an offer. Prince Aleksander, however, rejected all these offers.[27] He was at that time very fearful for the lives of his brothers Jakub and Konstanty, who had been kidnapped by the former Polish king Augustus II and held captive in Saxony. After their eventual release, he ceased political activity and left for Rome. In the Eternal City he joined the Arcadian academy, which is a gathering of writers, scholars and artists. He composed poetry and sponsored operas with music by Domenico Scarlatti and Filippo Juvarra.[28]

Aleksander's younger brother Konstanty, led the life of a lecher, roisterer and a ladies' man, engaging in affairs and never far from negative press. During his stay in Rome in 1700, his affair with the courtesan Tola di Leone was the talk of the town. Konstanty did not play a major political role after returning to the Polish-Lithuanian Commonwealth. The period of imprisonment at the hands of August II in the fortress Pleissenburg and then in Königstein resulted in a lasting negative effect on his mental health. Konstanty's relationship with Maria Józefa (Marie Josphe) née Wessel from 1704 to 1727, was marked by many disputes over property and was fraught

27 One possibility for this could be Aleksander's romantic view of marriage which took precedence over political and financial considerations. He had numerous romantic affairs with a number of high-ranking noblewomen, including the French Countess de Tournelle; Grand Hetmaness of the Polish-Lithuanian Crown, Elżbieta Sieniawska (neé Lubomirska); and Countess Maria Aurora von Königsmarck.

28 Aleksandra Skrzypietz, 'Sanctifying the sinner – the turbulent life of Prince Aleksander Sobieski', in Bogdan Rok and Filip Wolański, *Old Polish culture – searching for the sacred, finding the profane* [*Kultura staropolska – poszukiwanie sacrum odnajdywanie profanum*], (Toruń, 2018), 297–232.

with mutual distrust and jealousy.[29] While Konstanty himself had been taken into account as a candidate for her in 1708, it met with opposition from King Stanislaw Leszczynski and Tsar of Russia Peter I and any dreams he had had of the crown ended there.

***

The interest in being well connected with the Sobieskis, however, was still alive in the first half of the eighteenth century. The activity of queen-widow Maria Kazimiera d'Arquien Sobieska ensured that all her grand-daughters from the relationship of prince Jakub (James) and Jadwiga Elżbieta (Hedwig Elizabeth) were desirable as queens on European thrones. Similar plans for princesses were provided by the imperial court, including Empress-widow Eleonor and Empress Amalia Wilhelmina, proposing Maria Kazimiera to marry her daughters off to Italian princes – Francesco Maria d'Este and Rinaldo d'Este from Modena or Joseph Maria de Guastalla. They also looked for candidates in Parma – with Antonio Farnese among others counting on the favour of Cosimo III d'Medici. All of them, however, demanded too much dowry from their wives and, from the Sobieskis point of view, they were perceived as physically or mentally unfit. They also did not have the Emperor's consent to the marriage.[30]

29   Aleksandra Skrzypietz, *Rozkwit i upadek rodu Sobieskich*, (Warsaw, 2014), 299–305; idem, 'Marriage adventures of Prince Konstanty Sobieski', in Stanislaw Rosik and Przemysław Wiszewski, eds, *Cor hominis. Wielkie namiętności w dziejach, w źródłach i studiach nad przeszłością [Cor hominis. Great passions in history, in sources and studies of the past]*, (Wrocław, 2007), 325–342; Andrzej Sikorski, 'Maria Józefa née Wessel, wife of Prince Konstanty Sobieski', in *Rocznik Polskiego Towarzystwa Heraldycznego. Seria nowa*, Vol. 4, No. 15, (1999), 189–195.

30   Jean du Hamel du Breuil, 'Le mariage du Pretendant, Jacques Edovard Stuart avec Clementine Sobieska (1719)', in *Revue d'Histoire diplomatique*, (1895), 53–96; Gernot O. Gürtler, 'Die "Stuart-Sobieski-Connection". Dynastische Realpolitik oder diplomatische Mesaliance?', in *Annales Universitatis Mariae Curie-Skłodowska" Sectio F, Historia*, Vol. l, (1995), 103–119; Aleksandra Skrzypietz, 'Marriage problems of Maria Klementyna Sobieska', in Stanisław Achremczyk, ed., *Między Barokiem a Oświeceniem. Staropolski regionalizm*, (Olsztyn, 2008),

The damaged property and debts incurred by Prince Jakub, however, would cause a decline in significance for this once great house. The wealth of King Jan III Sobieski was by the early eighteenth century solely a myth. The entire territorial heritage had been divided between three sons and its parts were then lost piecemeal to Swedish, Russian and Saxon encroachments. In addition, the life of the prince at the court in Oława (Ohlau) in Silesia was consuming large sums of money. In a short time the Sobieski family became pawns of the European political scene. Difficulties were further exacerbated by the activities of European powers, including the emperor, who in 1719 protested against Maria Klementyna's (Maria Clementina's) relationship with the exiled James Francis Edward Stuart, referred to as the 'Pretender' to the kingdoms of Britain and Ireland.[31]

In the years 1710–1715 the queen-widow planned to marry the eldest of the sisters (also named Maria Kazimiera) to the elector Charles Philip Wittelsbach, which met with the approval of Pope Clement XI and Emperor Joseph I. The widow of Jan III soon abandoned these plans in order to bind her granddaughter to the James Stuart III. She believed that the end of the War of the Spanish Succession would allow him to regain the thrones of Britain and Ireland. Jakub Sobieski's strong objection, with the influence of the imperial court's discontent, ordered her to search among suitable candidates in France. At that time several candidates were involved such as Louis Armand Prince de Conti, the legitimate son of Louis XIV; Louis Alexander, Count of Toulouse; Louis August, Prince de Dombes; and Louis Charles, Count d'Eau. However, Prince Jakub believed, that from the point of view of the ongoing war between Saxony and Sweden, the marriage of Marie Casimire could be used as a political opportunity to form an alliance with King Charles XII. Negotiations in this respect lasted until 1718 but ended in failure. Unexpectedly, the prince returned to the prospect of the marriage of one of his daughters with James III, after the

---

230–245; Jarosław Pietrzak, 'Wife for the Pretender. Concerning the marriage between Maria Clementina Sobieska and James Francis Edward Stuart 1718–1720', in *Eastern European History*, (2019), 33–47.

31   Gaetano Platania, *La politica europea e il matrimonio inglese di una principessa polacca: Maria Clementina Sobieska* [*European politics and the English marriage of a Polish princess: Maria Clementina Sobieska*], (Rome, 1994), passim.

appearance of his representative, Charles Wogan, at the court in Oława. Support from the Queen of Spain, Elizabeth Farnese, and Pope Clement XI, made the prince decide to give his youngest daughter Maria Klementyna, thus acting against the custom of daughters in order of their seniority.[32]

Similarly, serious problems arose when attempting to find suitable matches for the remaining daughters. Maria Karolina (Marie Charlotte) was to be married in 1714 to the son of Tsar Peter I, Alexei, or with the Prince of Courland, Ferdinand. The queen-widow Maria Kazimiera objected to both of the ideas considering them inappropriate because of the age or bad manners of the candidates. It was not until 1722 that new plans for the marrying of the eldest daughter, Marie Casimire, to Duc de Bouillon Emanuel Theodose, and her younger sister Maria Karolina to the son of that prince, Frederic Maurice, were arranged. Prince Jakub was reluctant to give his consent. His reservation concerned the size of the daughters' dowries, the status of the de Bouillon family as the rulers of the Sedan, and the fact that one of the sisters would be mother-in-law to the second, which was considered immoral. The conversations involved the Austrians, the Spanish, the Bavarians and Prince Eugene of Savoy. The princess and the Duc de Bouillon, over the years 1722–1723, exchanged love correspondence, in which their feelings were guaranteed and loyalty was assured, but the plans ended with the unexpected death of queen-widow Maria Kazimiera in May 1723. At that time, full negotiations over the marriage contract of Maria Karolina were conducted, in which the princess gave up her rights to the Sobieski estates, while she was guaranteed a payment of 750,000 livres and her status as a blood princess at the French court secured by her grandmother in Paris. When Maria Karolina arrived in Strasbourg in 1723, she received a message that her fiancé had fallen from a horse and died shortly afterwards. Maria Karolina's plans fell through and her finances collapsed.

32   Aleksandra Skrzypietz, 'Around the marriages of the Sobieski princesses – from east to west Europe', in Filip Wolański and Robert Kołodziej, eds, *Staropolski ogląd świata. Rzeczpospolita między okcydentalizmem a orientalizacją. Przestrzeń wyobraźni* [*Old Polish view of the world. Rzeczpospolita between occidentalism and orientalization. Space of imagination*], (Toruń, 2009), 246–262; eadem, 'Two Marriages of Granddaughters of King John III', in *Historiae. Historica. Acta Facultatis Philosophicae Universitatis Ostraviensis*, Vol. 215, (2004), 39–48.

Probably for fear of returning to her father's court and the prospect of joining a convent, she agreed to marry her would-be husband, Charles Gotfrey d'Auvergen de Bouillon after a papal dispensation, but without the consent of Prince Jakub. Later, her husband's disagreeable lifestyle forced Maria Karolina, the last of the Sobieski family, to return to Poland around 1733, where she settled in the Ruthenian estates. Her bold plans for the marriage of her daughter – Maria Ludwika (Marie Louise) to one of the Polish magnates were not realised. Her father's death in 1737 closely followed by hers in 1740 closed the history of the great Sobieski family.[33]

The story of the Sobieskis is a story of political shrewdness, military prowess and strategic marriages. From their late medieval origins the leaders of the family displayed an astute ability to court power to their benefit and to build powerful marriage alliances which allowed them to take their place among the elite nobility of Rzeczpospolita. The glory won by Jan Sobieski at the head of his Winged Hussars at Vienna in 1683 will forever resonate in European history. His crowning as King Jan III of Poland-Lithuania shortly after his iconic victory became the pinnacle of achievement for the Sobieskis. Queen Maria Kazimiera proved to be more than equal to the task of governing the commonwealth in both domestic and international affairs. Her vision and activity influenced the very direction of European international relations at the time, supporting the interests of the Polish-Lithuanian Commonwealth. The subject of this collection of essays, Princess Maria Clementina, held the last hopes of her family regaining the chance of wielding royal power at a time when her family's fortunes had entered its twilight years. The Stuart claimant to the thrones of Britain and Ireland did not succeed in obtaining a restoration and, although the marriage brought renewed opportunities for a Stuart restoration through her sons Prince Charles Edward and Prince Henry Frederick for another generation, the final glimmer of both royal lines flickered out at the end of eighteenth century.

---

33   Aleksandra Skrzypietz, 'The Radzivills towards the heritage of the Sobieskis', in Rimantas Sliužinskas (sudarė), *Baltijos regiono istorija ir kultura; Lietuva ir Lenkija*, (Klaipėda, 2007), 55–71.

Bibliography

Books

Barker, Thomas M., *Double Eagle and Cresent. Vienna's Second Turkish Siege and its historical setting*, (New York, 1967).

Barycz, Henryk, *Rzecz o studiach w Krakowie dwóch generacji Sobieskich* [*The thing about studying in Krakow of two generations of Sobieski*], (Kraków, 1984).

Besala, Jerzy, *Stanisław Żółkiewski*, (Warszawa, 1988).

Chróścicki, Juliusz A., Flisowska, Zuzanna, and Migasiewicz, Paweł, eds, *I Sobieski a Roma. La famiglia reale polacca nella Città Eterna*, (Warsaw, 2018).

Czamańska, Ilona, *Wiśniowieccy. Monografia rodu* [*Wiśniowieccy. The monography of family*], (Poznań, 2007).

Czarniecka, Anna, *Nikt nie słucha mnie za życia ... Jan III Sobieski w walce z opozycyjną propagandą (1684–1696)* [*Nobody listens to me during my lifetime ... Jan III Sobieski in the fight against opposition propaganda (1684–1696)*], (*Warszawa*, 2009).

de Schryver, Reginald, 'Princess Teresa Kunegunda Sobieska 1676–1730. Thirty-five years of solitude', in Tatjana Soldatjenkova and Emmanuel Waegemans, eds, *For East is East: Liber Amicorum Wojciech Skalmowski*, (Leuven-Paris-Dudley, 2003).

Długosz, Jósef, *Jakub Sobieski 1590–1646. Parlamentarzysta, polityk, podróżnik i pamiętnikarz* [*Jakub Sobieski 1590–1646. Parliamentarian, politician, traveler and memoirist*], (Wrocław, 1989).

Fayard, Janine, *Attempts to build a 'Third Party' in North Germany 1690–1694*, Ragnhild Hatton, ed., *Louis XIV and Europe*, (Plymouth, 1976).

Góralski, Zbigniew, *Urzędy i dygnitarstwa w dawnej Rzeczypospolitej* [*Offices and dignities in old Poland*], (Warsaw, 1983).

Haratym, Andrzej, 'Jan Sobieski as the Crown Field Hetman (May 1666–February 1667)', in Mirosław Nagielski, ed., *Old Polish martial art of the 16th–17th century*, (Warsaw, 2002).

Hesse, Werner, *Hier Wittelsbach, hier Pfalz. Die Geschichte der pfälzischen Wittelsbacher von 1214—1803*, (Landau/Pfalz, 1986).

Kłaczewski, Witold, *Jerzy Sebastian Lubomirski*, (Wrocław, 2002).

Komaszyński, Michał, *Maria Kazimiera d'Arquien Sobieska (1641–1716) królowa Polski*, (Kraków, 1984).

Komaszyński, Michał, *Marie Casimire, reine de Pologne dernière résidente royale du Château de Blois*, (Katowice, 1995).

Kurtyka, Janusz, *Latyfundium Tęczyńskich. Dobra i ich właściciele [Tęczyński latifundium. Estates and owners]*, (Kraków, 1999).

Litwin, Henryk, *Napływ szlachty polskiej na ziemie ukrainne w latach 1569–1648 [The inflow of Polish nobility to Ukraine 1569–1648]*, (Warszawa, 2000).

Markuszewska, Aneta, *Festa i muzyka na dworze Marii Kazimiery Sobieskiej w Rzymie (1699–1714) [Festa and music at the court of Maria Kazimiera Sobieska in Rome (1699–1714)]*, (Warsaw, 2012).

Nagielski, Mirosław, *The Franco-Austrian rivalry in the Polish-Lithuanian Commonwealth during the late reign of Jan Kazimierz Waza*, in Ryszard Skowron, ed., *Poland in the face of great conflicts in modern Europe. On the history of diplomacy and international relations in the 15th–18th centuries [Polska w obliczu wielkich kofliktów w nowożytnej Europie. Studia z historii dyplomacji i stosunków międzynarodowych od XV do XVIII wieku]*, (Kraków, 2009).

Pietrzak, Jaroslaw, 'Because of these times I see very little genuine love. Marie Casimire's relationship with female members of the Sobieski family', in Anna Kalinowska and Paveł Tyszka, eds, *Maria Kazimiera Sobieska (1641–1716). W kręgu rodziny, polityki i kultury*, (Warsaw, 2017).

Platania, Gaetano, *Gli ultimi Sobieski e Roma. Fasti e miserie di una famiglia reale polacca tra Sei e Settecento (1699–1715)*, (Rome, 1989).

Platania, Gaetano, *La politica europea e il matrimonio inglese di una principessa polacca: Maria Clementina Sobieska*, (Roma, 1994).

Serwański, Maciej, 'Être une reine étrangère: deux Françaises en Pologne', in Isabelle Poutrin and Marie-Karine Schaub, eds, *Femmes et pouvoir politique. Les princesses d'Europe XVe-XVIIIe siècle*, (Rosny-sous-Bois, 2007).

Skrzypietz, Aleksandra, 'Around the marriages of the Sobieski princesses – from east to west Europe', in Filip Wolański and Robert Kołodziej, eds, *Staropolski ogląd świata. Rzeczpospolita między okcydentalizmem a orientalizacją. Przestrzeń wyobraźni [Old Polish view of the world. Rzeczpospolita between occidentalism and orientalization. Space of imagination]*, (Toruń, 2009).

Skrzypietz, Aleksandra, 'Foreign "language if we need it then" – "foreign" and "our" in the eyes of Sobieski', in Filip Wolański, ed., *Staropolski ogląd świata – problem inności [Old Polish view of the world – the problem of otherness]*, (Toruń, 2007).

Skrzypietz, Aleksandra, *Jakub Sobieski*, (Poznań, 2015).

Skrzypietz, Aleksandra, *Królewscy synowie – Jakub, Aleksander i Konstanty Sobiescy [The Royal sons – Jakub, Aleksander and Konstanty Sobieski]*, (Katowice, 2011).

Skrzypietz, Aleksandra, 'Marriage adventures of Prince Konstanty Sobieski', in Stanislaw Rosik and Przemysław Wiszewski, eds, *Cor hominis. Wielkie*

namiętności w dziejach, w źródłach i studiach nad przeszłością [*Cor hominis.*
  Great passions in history, in sources and studies of the past], (Wrocław, 2007).

Skrzypietz, Aleksandra, 'Marriage problems of Maria Klementyna Sobieska', in
  Stanisław Achremczyk, ed., *Między Barokiem a Oświeceniem. Staropolski
  regionalizm*, (Olsztyn, 2008).

Skrzypietz, Aleksandra, '"Regent" of Poland – facts and myths in the biography
  of Maria Kazimiera', in Bożena Czwojdrak and Agata A. Kluczek, eds,
  Kobiety i władza w czasach dawnych [*Women and power in ancient times*],
  (Katowice, 2015).

Skrzypietz, Aleksandra, *Rozkwit i upadek rodu Sobieskich* [*The flourishing and fall
  of the Sobieski family*], (Warsaw, 2014).

Skrzypietz, Aleksandra, 'Sanctifying the sinner – the turbulent life of Prince
  Aleksander Sobieski', in Bogdan Rok and Filip Wolański, *Old Polish culture –
  searching for the sacred, finding the profane* [*Kultura staropolska – poszukiwanie
  sacrum odnajdywanie profanum*], (Toruń, 2018).

Skrzypietz, Aleksandra, 'Two Marriages of Granddaughters of King John III', in
  Historiae. Historica. Acta Facultatis Philosophicae Universitatis Ostraviensis,
  Vol. 215, (2004).

Sobieski, Jan *Peregrynacja po Europie (1607–1613). Droga do Baden (1638)*
  [*Peregrination around Europe (1607–1613) Road to Baden (1638)*], Jósef
  Długosz, ed., (Warszawa-Wrocław-Kraków, 1991).

Spielman, John P. *Leopold I of Austria*, (New Brunswick-New Jersey, 1977).

Targosz, Karolina, *Jan III Sobieski mecenasem nauk i uczonych*, (Wrocław-
  Warszawa, 1991).

Targosz, Karolina, *Jana Sobieskiego nauki i peregrynacje* [*Jan Sobieski's education
  and peregrinations*], (Wrocław-Warszawa, 1985).

Trawicka, Zofia, *Jakub Sobieski 1591–1646. Studium z dziejów warstwy magnackiej
  w Polsce z czasów Wazów* [*Jakub Sobieski 1591–1646. A study on the history of
  the magnate in Poland in the era of Vasa dynasty*], (Kraków, 2007).

Trawicka, Zofia 'Wedding and funeral speeches by Jakub Sobieski', in Henryk
  Suchojad, ed., *Weddings, baptisms and funerals in the 16th-17th centuries.
  Culture of life and death* [*Śluby, chrzciny i pogrzeby w XVI I XVII wieku.
  Kultura życia i śmierci*], (Warszawa, 2001).

Ujma, Magdalena, *Latyfundium Jana Sobieskiego* [*Latifundium of Jan Sobieski*],
  (Opole, 2005).

Waliszewski, Kazimierz, *Marysieńka. Marie de la Grange d'Arquien Reine de
  Pologne femme de Sobieski 1641–1716*, (Paris, 1898).

Wójcik, Zbigniew, *Jan Sobieski, król Polski* [*Jan Sobieski, king of Poland*],
  (Warsaw, 1983).

Articles

Banach, Aandrzej Kazimierz, 'Conversions of Protestants to Catholicism in the Crown in 1560–1600', in *Seria Historica*, Vol. 77, (1985).

du Hamel du Breuil, Jean, 'Le mariage du Pretendant, Jacques Edovard Stuart avec Clementine Sobieska (1719)', in *Revue d'Histoire diplomatique*, (1895).

Gürtler, Gernot O., 'Die "Stuart-Sobieski-Connection". Dynastische Realpolitik oder diplomatische Mesaliance?', in *Annales Universitatis Mariae Curie-Skłodowska. Sectio F, Historia*, Vol. l, (1995).

Komaszyński, Michał, 'Die Beziehungen zwischen den Höfen der Wittelsbacher und dem von Sobieski in der zweiten Hälfte des XVII. Jahrhunderts', in *Zeitschrift für Bayerische Landesgeschichte*, Vol. 46, (1983).

Komaszyński, Michał, 'Die politische Rolle der bayerischen Kurfürstin Theresia Kunigunde', in *Zeitschrift für Bayerische Landesgeschichte*, Vol. 45, (1982).

Nagielski, Mirosław, 'Jan Sobieski – difficult beginnings of the career of the Turkish conqueror near Vienna', in *Biblioteka Epoki Nowożytnej*, Vol. 2, (2015).

Pietrzak, Jaroslaw, 'Genealogical and heraldic legend Sobieski family as a part of ancestral propaganda', in *Rocznik Polskiego Towarzystwa Heraldycznego*, Vol. 25, (2016).

Pietrzak, Jaroslaw, 'Wife for the Pretender. Concerning the marriage between Maria Clementina Sobieska and James Francis Edward Stuart 1718–1720', in *Eastern European History*, (2019).

Plewczyński, Marek, 'The military ancestors of Jan III Sobieski in the 16th century', in Janusz Wojtasik, ed., *Jan III Sobieski – wódz i polityk [Jan III Sobieski – commander and politician 1629–1696]*, (Siedlce, 1997).

Sikorski, Andrzej, 'Maria Józefa née Wessel, wife of Prince Konstanty Sobieski', in *Rocznik Polskiego Towarzystwa Heraldycznego. Seria nowa*, Vol. 4, No. 15, (1999).

Skrzypietz, Aleksandra, '"Great love is full of fear" – romance of Jan Sobieski and Maria Kazimiera', in *Biblioteka Epoki Nowożytnej*, Vol. 2, (2015).

Skrzypietz, Aleksandra, 'Prince Jakub Sobieski and his contacts with European courts after the outbreak of the Great Northern War', in *Wieki Stare i Nowe*, Vol. 4, No. 9, (2012).

Skrzypietz, Aleksandra, 'The Radzivills towards the heritage of the Sobieskis', in Rimantas Sliužinskas (sudarė), *Baltijos regiono istorija ir kultura; Lietuvair Lenkija*, (Klaipėda, 2007).

Skrzypietz, Aleksandra, 'Teofila Sobieska née Daniłłowicz – "not a female but male heart" woman', in *Wschodni Rocznik Humanistyczny*, Vol. 2, (2005).

Trawicka, Zofia, 'The extrajudicial political activity of Jakub Sobieski', in *Śląski Kwartalnik Historyczny Sobótka*, Vol. 35, (1980).

Wasilewski, Tadeusz, *Ludwika Karolina z Radziwiłłów* in *Polski słownik biograficzny*, Vol. 18, (1980).

Wimmer, Jan, 'Military traditions of the Sobieski family', in *Śląski Kwartalnik Historyczny Sobótka*, Vol. 35, No. 2, (1981).

RICHARD K. MAHER

3 The Rescue and Escape of Princess Maria Clementina Sobieska

It can be a rare occasion to find an episode of history as audacious and spectacular as the one described in the title of this paper. Accounts of the rescue and escape of Princess Maria Clementina Sobieska have been retold and reproduced in many forms over the years since the events themselves. Space considerations have ruled out the reproduction of one of the original accounts in this volume; it is, however, important to include *a* version of the events themselves to contextualise the other papers for our readers, but also to help bring the extraordinary events to renewed public attention. The author here offers a condensed but no less dramatic version which is based entirely on Sir Charles Wogan's *Mémoires sur l'enterprise d'Innsbruck en 1719*, which he had written and presented to Queen Marie Leszczyńska of France, cousin of Queen Clementina, in Paris on 4 March 1745. Cathy Winch translated and published this version in a bilingual format in 2008, which has been immensely useful in the preparation of this paper.[1] The paper is almost the same as was recounted on the occasion of the public seminar held on 30 April 2019 at Europe House

1   See chapter 3. For recent publications about the rescue see Winch, C., *The rescue of Clementina Stuart*, (Belfast, 2008); see also Canavan, T., 'Making a hole in the moon: the rescue of Princess Clementina' *History Ireland*, Vol. 1, No. 4, (winter 1993); Clare Lois Carroll, *Exiles in a global city: the Irish and early modern Rome, 1609–1783*, (Leiden, 2017), 232–256; see also Estelle Gittins, 'Jacobite relics in

in Dublin to commemorate the tercentenary of Clementina's rescue and escape, with minor stylistic adaptations suitable for its transmission in a printed format. The author forgoes the opportunity to expand and contextualise the events and provide an analysis of the various versions of the rescue here, but encourages interested readers to explore the various sources listed at the end of this chapter.[2] It must be added here that what follows is not a fitting substitute for the original on which it is based, but for the purposes of this publication, the author hopes the following is sufficient and enjoyable.

***

Princess Maria Clementina Sobieska must have felt a mixture of disbelief, sorrow and anger as she and her mother were escorted to their enforced confinement at the Palais Trapp in Innsbruck in September 1718. On the orders of Holy Roman Emperor Charles VI, ally of King George I of Britain and Ireland, the princesses had been arrested on their way through imperial territory to meet James Stuart III, George's direct rival, at Bologna in order to complete a marriage alliance between the royal houses of Stuart and Sobieski. Imperial guards were posted at all entrances to their lodgings and the Sobieski princesses were confined. It didn't take long before messages arrived by post and via their attendants informing them that an attempt was being planned to spirit Clementina across the Alps to her betrothed. Charles Wogan had played a key role in the marriage arrangements between his royal master James III and the Sobieski family. James now turned to him again knowing that he could count on his ingenuity and his determination. Wogan began making preparations to assist Clementina with his usual zeal.

Trinity College, Dublin' in *History Ireland Magazine*, Vol. 26, No. 1 (January/February 2018).

2   For a thorough comparative analysis of the literary motivations of the various accounts of the rescue which were collected and published by John T. Gilbert in his *Narratives of the Detention, Liberation and Marriage of Maria Clementina Stuart* in 1894, see Clare Lois Carroll, *Exiles in a global city: the Irish and Early Modern Rome, 1609–1783*, (Leiden, 2018), 232–256.

Wogan obtained false identification papers for his purposes from Pope Clement XI, godfather of Clementina. He obtained official permission from Clementina herself, and from her father Prince James Louis Sobieski to plan and carry out the rescue. Only these individuals, Papal Legate Cardinal Origo in Bologna (who doubted the attempt's feasibility), and a small number of trusted attendants were aware of the plot. Over many months, Wogan wove together the delicate strands of his plan and its secrecy was threatened many times, but he maintained his own incognito and his plan with impressive skill and successfully avoided detection by the ever-watchful agents of George I and of his ally Charles VI. He then travelled to Sélestat near Strasbourg on the eastern frontier of the Kingdom of France, where Arthur Dillon's Irish Regiment was stationed. From it, he recruited the rescue party. They were Major Richard Gaydon, Captain Luke O'Toole, Captain John Misset. Misset's wife Lady Eleanor, who was five months pregnant, accompanied him along with her young attendant Jeanneton. The gentlemen were all Hiberno-Norman Kildare Palesmen and kinsmen of Wogan. They were then joined by James Stuart's valet de chamber, Michel Vezzosi.

By 27 April 1719, the rescue party had moved into position at the Black Eagle Inn on the southern outskirts of Innsbruck on an atrocious night of icy winds, sleet and snow. The young French attendant of Lady Misset, Jeanneton, was to play the most important role of all, to trade places with Clementina and feign illness for as long as she could; but she hadn't been told of Clementina's true identity, lest it add to her apprehension. For this reason, she was told she was to trade places with a young countess who was, as the fib went, eloping with Captain O'Toole. She had been promised both safety and a reward in gold for the part she would play; however, when it came time to prepare Jeanneton for the role, the plans almost completely collapsed. Jeanneton was quite tall, and she was proud of it, and, believing it gave her an unusual point of distinction, she always wore heels to accentuate this feature. When Wogan and the rescue party told her that she was going to have to wear flat shoes, since Clementina was much shorter, Jeanneton obstinately refused. She became so implacable for half an hour that the group were in despair. At great length, it was a tearful Lady Misset who finally succeeded in persuading the young woman to wear the shoes despite her misgivings.

Finally, Wogan and Jeanneton left the Inn at 11.30 p.m. and they trudged through the atrocious weather and muddy streets. Jeanneton continued to curse the Ostrogoth shoes and the shabby English coat she had to wear, but they finally arrived at the house just after midnight. The weather was so bad that the guards had left their posts and taken shelter in an inn across the street. They had assumed that no one would attempt to abduct a royal princess in such awful weather conditions. With this good fortune, Jeanneton was in the door and up the stairs without any trouble. She was met by Clementina's chamberlain, Monsieur de Chateaudoux (an experienced attendant of Saint-Germain-en-Laye) at the top, who escorted her into the Princess's chambers. Clementina made her final preparations to leave and then bid her dear mother an agonised goodbye. She put on the heavy English coat and left a letter which gave the impression that her mother had nothing to do with the escape; but eventually Chateaudoux had to physically separate mother and daughter and help Clementina down the stairs. Wogan stood three doors down for an interminable half hour, until, after the clock had struck one, Clementina emerged onto the street and they set off towards the Black Eagle. The sleet was beating down so furiously that at one point on their way they encountered a substantial channel of water running across their path. Being in a rush to get across, Wogan directed the princess to step on a stone and reach the other side, but when the Princess stepped onto it, she sank into the muddy channel. This threw Wogan into much confusion as he helped the princess out of the water, but they pressed on. Her page Konski had caught up with them carrying a bundle of Clementina's effects, which he neglected to mention to Wogan had contained all of her priceless crown jewels. At about half one they arrived at the Inn where the harrowed rescue party were waiting. Addressing them all, the princess said, 'Welcome to you my brave rescuers … may the good God, who brought you to me, be our guide from now on.' While they prepared to leave, Konski, obviously terrified of the consequences he might face if he were seen there since he was staying behind in Innsbruck, simply flung the bundle behind the door in the room and quietly but speedily left without saying a word.

The party left the Inn at about 2 a.m.; Clementina, Lady Misset, Wogan and Gaydon in their carriage with Vezzosi on horseback in front of them, and O'Toole behind. They were ten minutes out the road when Clementina asked about her jewels, but Wogan didn't know what she was talking about. All the horses were ordered to halt. The whole party had to wait another excruciating half hour while O'Toole galloped back to the inn. Finding the front door unlocked, he quietly let himself in, and as discreetly as possible searched in the dark until at last, he found the bundle behind the door, and he rejoined the elated party where he had left them. They made slow progress on the steep road up Mt Brenner but reached the summit at dawn on 28 April, where captain Misset was waiting for them.

While they changed horses for the next phase of the journey, Clementina fainted. Panic ensued until Lady Misset used a bottle of Eau de Carmes,[3] the smell of which revived the princess, who said, 'Ah my little woman, and you my poor marmosets, take courage; there is nothing to worry about.' She used pet names after this point, Wogan became 'Papa Warner', the original name he used while incognito when he first met her at her home in Oława. Lady Misset permanently became her 'little woman'. The harsh weather which battered them on the north side of Mt Brenner gave way to much gentler and milder conditions on its southern face. They only stopped to change horses and kept moving, entertaining the princess with stories. The princess acclimatised very well to the discomforts she faced in the small carriage. Wogan, wishing to remain alert, fought sleep as best he could using snuff and tobacco, but at one point he dosed off with something in his hands which promptly clattered Clementina on the head. Frozen in fear and mortified all he could manage was to murmur that '... it will never happen again', but Clementina made light of it.

Calamity seemed to hover around the rescue party as they sped towards the safety of the Italian States. One serious incident occurred as the carriage was travelling on the old and narrow Roman road through the mountains. The road was bordered by a wall on one side and a sheer precipice on the other, down to the River Adige. At one point on this dangerous road, the driver was speeding as instructed but took a dangerous risk by attempting to overtake a merchant wagon which hugged the wall. Those in the carriage only felt a jolt, nothing more; but then O'Toole rode up

3   Eau de Carmes is still produced today.

and furiously whipped at the driver, cursing him in a hushed voice. Wogan emerged and asked what the matter was but he knew O'Toole was not easily rattled, and seeing his distress, waited until later to shield the princess from seeing his demeanour. Apparently, the two outer wheels of the princess's carriage had gone off the road and dangled over the edge of the cliff. O'Toole, riding behind, thought for a horrifying second that the princess and his dear friends were about to tumble off the edge and plummet to their deaths, when the driver urged the horses back towards the middle of the road after he passed the wagon and the outer wheel of the princess's carriage hit an old tree trunk which knocked it back onto the empty road.

Wogan instructed Misset and O'Toole to remain at Wellishmile[4] in anticipation of the Emperor's first move to attempt to recapture Clementina. The Irishmen were instructed to intercept any courier passing through the town, as they would likely be carrying orders to the governors of Trento and Roveredo for the arrest of Clementina and her party. The Irish officers' orders were not to kill, but to delay by any other means. Meanwhile the others were making slow progress. The Princess of Baden and her son, the young prince, were on the road just ahead of the rescue party – taking every fresh horse along the road ahead of them. There was a danger that the Badens would recognise Clementina if they encountered her on the road, since they had visited her at Innsbruck on their way to Loreto. They continued warily on their way.

In Wellishmile, Misset and O'Toole waited at the inn masquerading as travelling merchants keen to attend a local fair, and as expected, towards 2 a.m. that night, they spotted a courier arriving, his horse completely exhausted beneath him. O'Toole, who spoke German, cordially called out to him to come and sit with them and take a drink since he looked so tired and thirsty. The tired officer sat and complained about the lack of fresh horses and the bad road, while Misset *sneakily* spiked his wine with

4   I am grateful to Mr Alexander von Peez for his inquiry into this place name. There is no record of a town with this name on the escape route anymore. It is possible that the name of the town was changed in the intervening years. Possible other forms are Welschmuehle / Walhazmuehle. The term 'Walhaz' yields fascinating information reaching into antiquity relating to ancient people who inhabited the region. 'Muehle' can be translated as 'Mill'.

a powerful eau-de-vie made locally in Strasbourg, and poured the rest of it into a large water jug nearby. The officer drank down his wine, noting its peculiar strength. The Irishmen acknowledged this, saying that it was a local product, and cautioned him to water it down to mediate the strength, which he did liberally. As his wits became progressively annihilated, the disguised culprits made a show of their drinking prowess, and wanting to save face, of course, the courier had to at least attempt to keep up. Within the hour, the poor man was completely incoherent and soon very ill. The Irishmen quietly removed his orders from his satchel and destroyed them, all the while consoling their new friend and helping him up to bed, where he could do no harm at all.

Later that morning on 29 April, the rescue party reached the town of Trento as the Badens were leaving, and as before, there was not a single fresh horse to be found for the next stage of the journey. Princess Clementina was obliged by the circumstances to remain in her coach while the sun's heat increased throughout the morning, since many notables of Trento had visited her at Innsbruck. The local people were mystified by this strange situation, a carriage full of gentlefolk sitting in their carriage, and they began to chance glances at who was inside. The group had to act quickly, so they came up with a plan to trick the governor, Prince de la Tour Taxis. Fortunately, the prince was indisposed due to an attack of gout, and Vezzosi was sent to his residence on behalf of the Count de Cernes and his family to ask for some horses to be released from fieldwork so that the count might catch the Badens. After an initial refusal, Vezzosi returned to say that the count was on his way to make a personal application to the prince. The prince was unwilling to embarrass the count by a further refusal, so he relented, and the party were moving again by 1 p.m., with just two field horses swapped for the two most tired.

They pushed on to Roveredo where they made a simple meal of bread and tea to sustain Clementina who had felt faint again. There were no fresh horses there either, so they had to continue with the same tired horses towards Alla, the last town of the emperor's territory, leaving Roveredo at about half past three. A detachment of mounted imperial dragoons gave them a moment's fright, but they passed them at a gallop without paying the slightest heed. A few hours later they were almost halfway to Alla when the carriage struck a stone on the road followed by a loud crack and the carriage came to sudden halt. Wogan got out to check the carriage only to find that the axel shaft had broken in two! He had only descended when behind him there was a shrill cry. He looked back to see Clementina, who'd lost her footing descending from the carriage, knee deep in a stream rushing by the roadside. She was pulled out easily though, and lady Misset helped her change. An attempt by Wogan and Vezzosi to replace the axel only brought them a little further along until it broke again at about 10 p.m. The party were forced to continue in the darkness on foot with the horses until they reached Alla. As they entered the town it was clear to them that they had finally caught up with the Badens and the town was busy with activity. They found lodging away from the fuss where Clementina could refresh herself; meanwhile Wogan searched high and low around Alla for any type of carriage that would allow them to keep travelling. The only thing he could find was a shoddy two-seater vehicle which he himself labelled 'a most wretched conveyance'. Wogan wrote that 'it was in this ridiculous contraption and predicament, that the cousin of Emperor Charles VI, and of the Queen of Spain, and grand-daughter of King Jan Sobieski III, left Alla at 2 a.m. on 30 April.' It was ten miles from Alla to the Venetian town of Peri, and so the weary group set out slowly and quietly. Gaydon twisted his ankle on the road and advised Wogan to move on and that he would wait at the roadside for Vezzosi to arrive with the Berlin carriage fully repaired. Onward they went. The exhausted Wogan walked alongside the two ladies in their conveyance. They were watching for a part of the road where it was bordered on either side by thick walls, as it demarcated the territories of Trentino of the Holy Roman Empire, and that of Venice ... and after some hours walking they perceived with quiet joy what they were waiting for. Once the little chariot passed the walls, they knew they had entered friendly territory, and Clementina, Wogan and Lady Misset sang out a *Te Deum* in thanks for their safe conduct to Venetian territory.[5] On Sunday 30th April, the three companions arrived at Peri at about 8

---

5   The public seminar which took place at Europe House in Dublin to celebrate the tercentenary of Clementina's rescue and escape was held on 30 April 2019, 300 years ago to the day that the rescue mission succeeded and Clementina escaped imperial territory.

a.m. to the sound of ringing church bells. The small church in Peri was holding an early service in honour of the Princess of Baden, who they knew would be passing through the town on her way to Verona. Clementina had the chariot driven straight to the church where she attended the service, careful to remain veiled.

They took a small room in a local inn where they arranged for dinner to be served at 2 p.m., and finally Clementina and Lady Misset were able to go comfortably asleep while Wogan awaited the arrival of his friends. At 1 p.m. the rest of the rescue party rode in, carriage and all, safe and sound; and at 2 p.m. the whole party was reunited and sat down to dinner together. Wogan wrote that 'the sudden meeting of the whole company together after so many mishaps and adventures and in a safe country created in everyone a feeling of pure and perfect joy the likes of which is hardly ever found in life.' They arrived at Verona at dusk on 30 April, and all of them slept a full night soundly and peacefully for the first time in four days.

They made for Bologna, avoiding the imperial territory of Mantua, by taking the road through Pepoli and Caprara, until they crossed the Po at Stellata. They arrived in Bologna on 2 May and took lodgings at the Pilgrim Inn at 11 a.m. The inn was crammed full of boisterous English gentlemen who couldn't help themselves commenting on Clementina's loveliness, which to Wogan displayed a complete lack of manners, he commented sourly, 'The English feel that in Italy they can behave in whatever way they like.' This situation wouldn't do, so Wogan paid a visit to his friend Cardinal Origo. The Kildareman decided to play a trick on him, since the cardinal had doubted that he would succeed in his plans to rescue Clementina. He called on the papal legate with a solemn expression, upon seeing which Origo said, 'Monsieur Wogan, I have known you for long time as a very accomplished gentleman: I was expecting to find you as a man of your word.' To which Wogan replied, 'In what way have I failed your eminence?' The cardinal replied shortly, 'The Princess Sobieski!' Wogan allowed a slow smile to creep across his face, 'She is here, Monsignor: and I am a man of my word.' The cardinal leapt out of his chair and exclaimed the words 'Qui! Qui!' banging his hands off the walls as he did. He made such a racket that his attendants ran into the room white-faced thinking he was being attacked.

The cardinal agreed to obtain quieter lodgings for Clementina and her beloved marmosets, and he had a small house near the city walls prepared for her. It was thought best to keep her identity secret, in order to maximise the effect of her arrival in Rome on the envoys of George I and Charles VI. This need for secrecy unwittingly led to a bit of controversy for the honourable Cardinal. He visited Clementina every evening between 9–11 p.m. and in order to keep the secret of her identity, he would ask his retinue to remain on the street while he continued the final 200 yards on foot and alone, with only a dark lantern to guide his way to the house. The Bolognese being none the wiser made the assumption that their beloved and pious Cardinal had succumbed to the fruits of Eve, and that he was visiting a mistress near the walls of the town.

James Stuart had travelled to Spain to lead a military expedition to Britain aimed at his restoration to his ancestral thrones and for that reason he was not there to welcome Clementina in person at Bologna. He had left powers and instructions with his chief minister, James Murray, to carry out a marriage-by-proxy in the event that Clementina escaped captivity. On 9 May, Clementina was married by proxy to James Stuart III. His representative, James Murray, had arrived with his sister Lady Marjorie the day before with a much more suitable carriage with which to convey Clementina to Rome. They set out on 10 May stopping along the way as they deemed appropriate or entertaining. As they approached the city on 15 May, they stopped near the Pontemolle on the Tiber where they remained until 4 p.m., while Cardinals Aquaviva, Gualtiero and many other high notables of the church came to pay their respects to Clementina. At 5 p.m. on 15 May 1719, Maria Clementina Sobieska Stuart crossed the bridge onto the avenue of the Porta del Popolo and into Rome as Queen *de Jure* of Britain and Ireland. Wogan wrote, 'The entry to Rome was a veritable Triumph.' The avenue was lined on both sides by the fine carriages of the Roman nobility and her passage was greeted with the cheers and acclamations of all who witnessed. Clementina took lodgings and remained at the Ursuline Convent with her little woman Lady Misset until James Stuart returned to Italy. He met his royal consort for the first time near Montefiascone, north of Rome, where they completed an official marriage ceremony on 1 September, at which Wogan acted as a witness.[6] King James knighted Wogan and granted him a baronetcy. The king knighted Misset, O'Toole and Gaydon, and provided brevets of advancement to be used to obtain promotion in the military service of any of the Catholic powers of Europe. James recognised Lady Misset's important role and honoured her by granting a brevet of advancement for her father who was also an officer in Dillon's regiment. In recognition of the incredible feat of leading the rescue mission to its success, Pope Clement XI bestowed Rome's highest civilian mark of distinction on Charles Wogan by having him made a Senator of Rome. Wogan, in recognition of the contribution made by his compatriots Richard Gaydon, Luke O'Toole and John Misset, requested that his excellency the pope extend the same honour to them, since they shared an equal part of the danger. On 15 June 1719, the four Irishmen were received on the Capitol to the sounding of ancient Roman trumpets and to the applause of all in attendance and were created Senators of Rome. Clementina produced two princes with James, Prince Charles Edward and Prince Henry Benedict, and the hopes of a Jacobite restoration were restored for another generation.

Bibliography

Corp, Edward, *The Jacobites at Urbino: an exiled court in transition*, (London, 2009)
Winch, Cathy, *The rescue of Clementina (Stuart): a 1719 adventure of the Irish Brigades, by Charles Wogan*, (Belfast, 2008).

6   Wogan records the date of the marriage as 2 September, but on the marriage certificate it is recorded as 'die prima Septembris', the source of this confusion is that the marriage took place at midnight on 1 September 1719. See Edward Corp, *The Jacobites at Urbino: an exiled court in transition*, (Basingstoke, 2009), 138.

Further Reading

Canavan, Tony, 'Making a hole in the moon: the rescue of Princess Clementina', in *History Ireland*, Vol. 1, No. 4, (1993).

Flood, Joseph, *The life of Chevalier Wogan: an Irish soldier of fortune*, (Dublin, 1922).

Female Fortitude, exemplify'd, in an impartial narrative, of the seizure, escape, and marriage of the Princess Clementina Sobiesky, as it was particularly set down by Mr. Charles Wogan ... who was the chief manager in that whole affair. Originally published in London, 1722. Published by Eighteenth Century Collections Online Print Editions, USA.

Gilbert, John T., *Narratives of the detention, liberation and marriage of Maria Clementina Stuart*, (Dublin, 1894); ibid, repr. (Dublin, 1970).

Huntly McCarthy, Justin, *The King over the water: or, the marriage of Mr. Melancholy*, (New York, 1911).

Lois Carroll, Clare, *Exiles in a global city: the Irish and Early Modern Rome, 1609–1783*, (Leiden, 2018).

Mason, Alfred E., *Clementina*, (London, 1901).

Miller, Peggy, *A wife for the Pretender*, (London, 1965).

RICHARD K. MAHER

4 Service and Exile: *Sir Charles Wogan, 1715–1719*

As the light was fading from his eyes in July 1754, one wonders what thoughts and emotions may have come to Sir Charles Wogan. In his latter years he had been honoured by his hosts in the Kingdom of Spain with the governorship of La Mancha, and then promoted to the governorship of Barcelona; achievements of which an Irish gentleman from County Kildare could indeed be proud. Regarding his activities on behalf of the exiled King James Stuart III though, his undoubted pride might have been tinged with other emotions. He wrote in 1746 that he had lost his inheritance in Ireland through 'the wildness of my youth' referring to his service to James.[1] Between 1715 and 1719, as this paper will show, he brought a level of energy, zeal and ingenuity which was badly needed by the unfortunate and beleaguered royal House of Stuart. For a man who possessed such clear talents and had earned the trust and esteem of his monarch the future held much promise. His most outstanding achievement, the rescue of the betrothed Princess Maria Clementina Sobieska on behalf of his liege, should have paved the path to high distinctions of royal favour and positions of authority at the king's side at the Jacobite court in exile in Rome, but this did not transpire. This paper provides an account of Wogan's activities in the early days of James III's exile from the Kingdom of France. Furthermore, it will juxtapose his previous service, his achievement of the rescue, the honours he received, and explore the

---

1   Hayes, R., *Irish swordsmen of France*, (Dublin, 1934), 299.

reasons for Wogan's apparent fall from grace in the aftermath of his most brilliant service for the Jacobite cause.

Wogan's Family Background and Formative Years

The Irish branch of the Wogan family had supported Charles I during the Wars of the Three Kingdoms (1638–1660), and they had resisted the Cromwellian campaign in Ireland (1649–1653). They had rallied to the colours of James II during the War of the Two Kings (1688–1691). Familial loyalty to the Stuart dynasty, as in former times, now found new expression through Charles Wogan. The date of his birth has been the source of some confusion among scholars, but stronger evidence suggests the year 1685.[2] At some point in the early eighteenth century, he was sent to England. The details of where he stayed or with whom he stayed remain obscure but recent scholarship by Cathy Winch asserts that in 1705 Wogan lived in Binfield, Berkshire, and there met and became friends with Alexander Pope.[3] The Wogan family owned a substantial 424 hectare estate in Norfolk,[4] inherited through marriage

2   See Wogan to John Hay, 18 January 1725, in Henrietta Tayler, *Jacobite Epilogue: a further selection of letters from Jacobites among the Stuart Papers at Windsor published by the gracious permission of his majesty the king*, (London, 1941), 293; see also Frank D'Arcy, 'Exiles and strangers: the case of the Wogans', in Gerard O'Brien, ed., *Parliament, politics and people; essays in eighteenth-century Irish history*, (Dublin, 1989), 182, where he cites his Spanish military service record, in which his age in the year 1731 is given as 47; also see Hugh A. Law, 'Sir Charles Wogan', *The Journal of the Royal Society of Antiquaries of Ireland*, Seventh Series, Vol. 7, No. 2 (31 December 1937), 257–258.

3   Cathy Winch, *The rescue of Clementina (Stuart)*, (Belfast, 2008), 16.

4   Originally built in the sixteenth century, the large house and estate were owned by the Gawdy family of Redenhall, Norfolk. In 1666 the house and estate passed by marriage to the Wogan family whose main holdings were in Pembrokeshire since their arrival from Normandy. The Wogans retained this large estate in Norfolk until 1778. See Alphonse O'Kelly de Galway, *Mémoire Historique et Généalogique sur la Famille de Wogan*, (Paris, 1896), 1, 35; For a more detailed description of the

in the mid-seventeenth century, so it is possible that the young Charles Wogan was financially supported and housed by his relatives in England. As Frank Darcy observed, the source of Wogan's education remains a mystery.[5] It must have been broad enough for him to acquire Latin and France along with an ability to communicate effectively in English, as the large body of his letters and poetry indicate.[6] He also seems to have had an in-depth knowledge of classical literature and history. Between these formative years and his later participation in the Jacobite rebellion of 1715, it is almost certain that Wogan went to France and joined Arthur Dillion's Irish Regiment.

Wogan's Involvement during 'the Fifteen'

Charles and his younger brother Nicholas were involved in the planning and launching of the rebellion in Scotland and England in the late autumn of 1715.[7] Upon the death of Queen Anne in 1714, the Whigs sought an acceptable replacement who would defend the protestant interest and they offered the crown to George, Elector of Hanover. As George I had but a distant Stuart connection in his lineage, many in Britain and Ireland considered him an illegitimate successor to the thrones of those kingdoms. Of twelve gentlemen who had assembled in London, confirmed their plans, and set off to northern England disguised as tourists to stoke rebellion, four of them were Irish. They were Colonel Henry Oxburgh (a veteran of the wars of Louis XIV), Charles and Nicholas Wogan, and James Talbot (also a veteran of the French

---

      house and estate, see Rachel Klausner, *A brief history of Gawdy Hall and its occupants*, (Harleston, 2004).

5   D'Arcy, 'Exiles and strangers', 182.

6   For Wogan's proficiency in Latin, the author refers to *The Wogan Manuscript*, housed at the Galway, Kilmacduagh, & Kilfenora Diocesan Archives.

7   There has been confusion about this but according to Frank D'Arcy it was indeed his younger brother Nicholas. See D'Arcy, 'Exiles and Strangers', 187.

service).[8] They travelled to the major houses of northern England and upon obtaining the support they sought, formed military units under the overall command of General Thomas Forster. Charles was Forster's *aide de camp*[9] while Nicholas commanded the fifth troop of the English Jacobite army in Northumberland.[10] The army was joined and strengthened by the Scottish Jacobite army under the command of John Erskine, Earl of Mar, who had raised the royal standard of the house of Stuart in Scotland. The joint forces pressed south from Kelso and marched towards Manchester but were met at Preston by six regiments of George I's army on 12 November. The battle has been treated in detail[11] elsewhere, but the Wogan brothers distinguished themselves thereat. A rare account of the battle housed at the Harris Museum in Preston asserts that the advance party defending the town from the bridge was commanded by a Captain Wogan.[12] During the battle Nicholas would save the life of the Hanoverian Captain Preston who had been wounded and threatened with execution by his Jacobite captors. The battle ended with the defeat of the Jacobite army, and the Wogans along with the other officers were marched as prisoners to London.

8   Robert Patten, *The history of the rebellion in the year 1715: with original papers, and the characters of the principal noblemen and gentlemen concern'd in it*, (London, 1717), 19.

9   Patten, *The history of the rebellion*, 50.

10 Ibid., 110.

11 Daniel Szechi, *1715, the Great Jacobite rebellion*, (Bury, 2006), 170–198.

12 *Harris Library, Preston, Community History Pamphlet Collection*, item number LE75 LET, no author, '*A Letter about the occurrences in the way to, and at Preston, by a gentleman who was an eyewitness to the said transactions*'.

Escape from Newgate

Approximately seventy Jacobite prisoners were paraded through London on the way to Newgate; however, far from being met with hostility there, upon arrival their bindings were removed and they were all treated to glasses of French wine![13] It may have been the case that the governor, Mr Pitts, empathised with the rebels' cause. Conditions were quite relaxed at Newgate. Wogan was allowed to engage in a poetic correspondence with a Northumbrian Jacobite gentleman, William Tunstall.[14] The prisoners were allowed frequent visits from friends and family from whom they could receive gifts; correspondence to and from the prison was unrestricted; benefactors from abroad could send funds to support the prisoners[15]; with their funds the prisoners could pay turnkeys to have their shackles removed, enjoy a variety of food and wine, and in Forster's case, to be housed and fed in the governor's residence itself.[16]

After the execution of James Radcliffe, third Earl of Derwentwater, and William Gordon, sixth Viscount Kenmuir, a Whiggish commentator quipped that their *Jacobite courage* did quickly appear then in its proper colours', and the rebels started to make escape plans.[17] On 7 April 1716, bills of high treason were found against Forster, Oxburgh, the two Wogans along with several other Jacobite leaders. Time being short, Forster escaped his loose confinement on 10 April. On 26 April, the night before his trial, Charles escaped Newgate by rushing the guards and forcing his way out

13 Daniel Defoe, *The history of the Press Yard*, (London 1717), 65.

14 Richard K. Maher, 'Poems from the prison yard; poetic correspondence between Charles Wogan and William Tunstall', in *History Ireland*, Vol. 25, No. 2, (March/April 2017).

15 Correspondence has survived between Wogan and Cardinal Gualtiero during his time at Newgate in which Wogan asks the cardinal to send him money. The correspondence itself indicates that Wogan had already been an acquaintance of the cardinal, which probably occurred at the Jacobite court in exile then at St Germain. See National Library of Ireland (hereafter N.L.I.), P519, n. 792–793.

16 Defoe, *History of the Press Yard*, 78.

17 Anonymous, *The secret history of the rebels in Newgate*, (London, 1717), 7.

with a party of other prisoners who dashed away into the darkened streets.[18] Some were retaken shortly afterwards but Wogan made his escape, the details of which are contained in his later correspondence with Jonathan Swift. After evading capture in parks and on rooftops around London, he headed south with a bounty of £500 on his head.[19] He took refuge under the walls of Arundel castle, before obtaining transport from a sympathiser from Chichester to Courcelles-sur-Seine within easy reach of Paris. He arrived there 'towards the end of June' in 1716.[20]

Return to James III's Service

Wogan was swiftly taken back into the service of James III once he arrived safely in France. Henrietta Taylor asserted that between 1716 and 1718 Wogan had served for two years in the Irish Regiment of Arthur Dillon in the French Service, but this was not precisely the case.[21] Indeed, this author seeks to clarify the nature of his connection with the regiment at a later stage but accepts that Wogan probably served in Dillon's prior to the 1715 rebellion. According to surviving correspondence from that year, Wogan was well-thought of for his role in the ill-fated rebellion of 1715 and for assisting other senior Jacobite prisoners in escaping Newgate.[22] He was asked to travel to Lyon and to take up residence there under a false identity where he would act as a conduit for Jacobite correspondence between Paris and the Italian states. This is a clear indication of James' trust in him and confidence in his abilities. From November 1716 until February 1717, Wogan was in Lyons, and a letter to him from Mar states that the king required him to follow him on the road to his new residence

18   Galway, Kilmacduagh & Kilfenora Diocesan Archives, *The Wogan Manuscript*, 6.
19   *The Wogan manuscript*, 4.
20   Winch, *The rescue of Clementina*, 47.
21   Henrietta Tayler, *Jacobite epilogue*, (London, 1941), 278.
22   Gordon to Paterson, Paris, 8 July 1716, *Calendar of Stuart Papers*, vol. 2, (Historical Manuscripts Commission), (London, 1904), 261.

in Bologna.[23] James had been forced to leave French territory as a stipu-
lation of the Treaty of Utrecht and he sought to establish his new court
in exile in the Papal States, eventually settling in the Palazzo Ducale in
Urbino at the behest of Pope Clement XI.

From the evidence presented above, it is certain that Wogan had returned to serve James III as a special agent in the summer of 1716. He was
based in Lyons between November of that year and February 1717 before
following James to his court. Thereafter, Wogan's trail may be picked up
again in correspondence between John Patterson and the earl of Mar, dated
5 June 1717, in which Wogan is mentioned as having set out in the company of Lieutenant-General Arthur Dillon from Paris to Rome.[24] This may
well explain the origin of the notion that Wogan had served in Dillon's
regiment. Even though he accompanied Dillon, it is unlikely that it was
in a soldiering capacity. It is more likely that Wogan was still serving as
James's agent, and that he had been sent to Paris in that capacity on special business.[25] Thereafter it seems that Wogan acted as security officer at
the Jacobite court in Urbino between completing special tasks given him
by James III. One such task included a diplomatic mission headed by the
2nd duke of Ormonde to negotiate a peace treaty between Charles XII
of Sweden and Peter I of Russia. Ultimately the aim had been to build an
alliance between the two powers against George I of Great Britain and
Ireland, also elector of Hanover.[26] Then in early 1718 he was given the commission to visit various courts to identify suitable princesses who might
be considered as potential brides for James III and he remained there after

---

23   Mar to Wogan, Avignon, 1 February 1717, *Calendar of Stuart Papers*, Vol. 2, 496.
      It appears that assassins had been intercepted *en route* to Avignon and that was
      the reason for the relocation of James's court to Bologna. See also Edward Corp,
      The Jacobites at Urbino, an exiled court in transition, (New York, 2008), 20; see also
      Frank McLynn, *The Jacobites*, (London, 1985), 162.

24   Patterson to Mar, 5 June 1717, *Calendar of Stuart Papers*, Vol. 4, (London,
      1910), 319.

25   As has been shown above, James III was not permitted to travel in the Kingdom
      of France; however, his mother (Mary of Modena) was terminally ill at the time
      of Wogan's visit, so it may be the case that Wogan was sent by James to see her and
      deliver a personal message from him.

26   Rebecca Wills, *The Jacobites and Russia, 1715–50*, (Dundern, 2002), 57.

his return from the mission.[27] The time spent at Urbino appears to have been quiet and peaceful (perhaps boring and tedious at times) with the exception of one embarrassing episode which occurred in July 1718. Wogan got into a quarrel with his housemate, another Irish officer named Major Donald McMahon. The quarrel could not be settled amicably so the men went out and fought a duel in the street.[28] It was the talk of the normally tranquil Italian town and James III was justifiably furious, conscious of how his enemies could use such evidence of dysfunction at his court in their propaganda. The Irishmen were reprimanded and confined to quarters. This would be the first time Wogan felt the chill wind of his liege's displeasure, but it would not be the last.

Wogan's Role in Princess Clementina's Betrothal and Rescue

Wogan was more than adept at travelling incognito, retaining it perfectly throughout his mission of 1718 to visit the royal courts of Europe to seek a potential bride for James. It was he who successfully arranged the marriage match between his king and Princess Maria Clementina Sobieska. As has been shown above by Dr Jarosław Pietrzak, the Sobieskis were one of the most notable royal houses in Europe. The match offered powerful connections, increased financial resources and no small amount of prestige. While Wogan laid the preparations for the match, James Murray was chosen to conclude the negotiations for the marriage contract. This annoyed Wogan, who allowed his irritation to be known, even though Murray's appointment to the task appeared to be largely political since, as he was a Protestant, it couldn't be said by James III's Whig detractors that he was overly favouring his Catholic subjects. Wogan's balking at

27   Mar to Ormonde, Friday 22 July 1718, *Calendar of Stuart Papers*, Letter of Francesco Bianchini to James III, 16 June 1719, vol. 7, (London, 1923), 73. Therein, passing reference is made to Wogan having taken trips into the countryside around Rome in the recent past.
28   Ibid, the letter describes the circumstances surrounding this duel in full detail.

a royal decision probably annoyed James. While at Ohlau fulfilling his duties, Murray seems to have spoken loosely about the marriage arrangement which resulted in the news being communicated by British spies to Vienna and in turn to London. Princess Clementina and her mother were detained and confined at Innsbruck *en route* to Bologna to meet James III in September 1718. Unable to directly influence the situation, James III left Bologna and travelled to Spain where a new attempt at a restoration was being prepared by James Butler, 2nd Duke of Ormond.

Wogan stepped forward and offered to plan a rescue mission for Clementina and was given permission to do so. He travelled between Rome, Bologna, Vienna, Ohlau and Strasbourg, successfully maintaining secrecy and laying plans for the rescue. He recruited members of Arthur Dillon's Irish Regiment in France to assist with the rescue. They were Captain John Misset, Captain Luke O'Toole and Major Richard Gaydon. All were Kildare Palesmen with traditional loyalty to the Stuarts and they seem to have been relatives of Wogan.[29] They were accompanied by Lady Eleanor Misset, who would act as a lady-in-waiting to Clementina, and Lady Misset's personal attendant Jeanneton. In spectacular fashion, the rescue party succeeded, much to the astonishment of James and his court in exile, and much to the fury of the British government.[30] While still on the road to Rome with the liberated princess, James III wrote to Wogan ordering him to travel to Spain to link up with he and John Hay, but Wogan refused to do so. This was very out of character for Wogan who generally seems to have been sensitive to protocol. Indeed, as a military man, to disregard an order is dangerous. His refusal is not to be treated lightly, given what came afterwards. Clementina had grown fond of Wogan and affectionately called him Papa Warner after first meeting him when he was using that name to mask his true identity. She asked him to remain with her and Wogan perhaps felt honour-bound to remain with his new queen; however, to refuse his king's request to join him on the cusp of an attempt at a restoration to

29   D'Arcy, 'Exiles and strangers', 177.
30   For the events of the rescue, see chapter 3.

his ancestral kingdoms must have aggravated James.[31] In his memoire of the rescue and escape which he wrote in 1745 and dedicated to the Queen of France (Marie Leszczyńska, a relative of Clementina) Wogan observed tersely that 'perhaps it would have been better for [my] fortune if [I] had obeyed'.[32] Maybe in the afterglow of such astounding success on his part, he desired to accompany his new queen to Rome and receive what praise and esteem would surely be accorded him. They wouldn't be unsubstantial as it turned out, but his pride would carry a price of its own.

The Stuart Court and the Eternal City

Princess Clementina arrived in Rome at 5 p.m. on 15 May 1719 to a triumphant welcome. She was met on the road near the Pontomolle on the Tiber by Cardinals Gualtiero & Aquaviva and other senior members of the church before crossing the bridge onto the avenue of the Porta del Popolo as Queen *de Jure* of Britain and Ireland. Roman nobles lined their carriages along the avenue and welcomed the young queen as she passed. Pope Clement XI, her godfather and namesake, received her in audience the following day allowing senior clerics to pay tribute to her.[33] From that point onwards, it appears that Clementina's sense of happiness and contentment diminished rather quickly.

In the absence of the king, the running of the Jacobite court in exile had been entrusted to James Murray. A man whose star had been rising, Murray enjoyed a level of favour with James III which seems to have surpassed all others and which endured for many years. This seems not to have been a positive development for the Jacobite cause. Murray incurred the hostility of Robert Harley, Earl of Oxford, who wrote of him a few years

31   By this time, James had already been told of the loss of the Spanish fleet bound for Britain and probably requested Wogan to go to Spain to assist him in his efforts to forge ahead with the restoration attempt.
32   Winch, *The rescue*, 143.
33   Winch, *The rescue*, 143 & 145.

prior to 1719, 'I am afraid this vain creature will create more mischief and do more harm to the king's service than all his family and he can ever be capable to retrieve.'[34] This was an icy indictment of the young man, but a premonition which held true with bitter consequences for many who came into contact with him. By May 1719 Murray had undermined and supplanted his mentor John Erskine, Earl of Mar, and in Mar's absence had replaced him as James III's acting secretary of state. In that capacity Murray had been left in charge of the administration of the court while the king was in Spain. The authority bestowed on him included representing the king as his proxy at the marriage ceremony carried out in Bologna after Clementina arrived there; reading and answering the king's correspondence; overseeing the administration of the court in exile; and after Clementina's arrival, the introduction of members of the Jacobite court to the young queen. By the time Clementina had arrived he had already vexed a large number of James' courtiers.

On the matter of introductions to members of the court, Murray made huge errors of judgement. He isolated Clementina, only allowing members of his own inner circle to attend her, which included Wogan and his companions for now. The narrative of events written in 1720 by Alexander Ford, 4th Lord Pitsligo, provides valuable insights into the events of June 1719 and subsequent period. According to the narrative, while at a local coffee house Murray announced to James III's adherents that Wogan would make the introductions but the news was viewed as a new piece of ill-treatment and that 'some complained of it aloud and short words passed on both sides'.[35] The strong reaction from James's adherents indicates the level of annoyance and dislike Murray had incurred by his behaviour at the time. Pitsligo further noted that Murray 'carried higher

34 Henrietta Tayler, *The Jacobite court at Rome, 1719*. Publications of the Scottish Historical Society, Third Series, vol. 31, (Edinburgh, 1938), *Part I*, 6, 7.

35 Pitsligo to James III, Rome, n.d. June 1719, in *The narrative of Lord Pitsligo: a narrative by Lord Pitsligo containing some anecdotes of the secret history of the Court of James in Italy, during his Lordship's residence there in the year 1719*, preserved in manuscript form at Fettercairn House, Kincardineshire, Scotland, quoted in full from Tayler, *The Jacobite Court at Rome, 1719*, Part I, 60–61.

every day, even before he executed the Proxie[36] [sic], but that affair made
him quite forget himself, a thing too natural to mankind'.[37] In terms of
court protocol, the members of the court were not wrong to complain, as it
was the norm for members of equal or higher rank to make introductions
of this kind and Wogan held no noble title as yet. In the end, and after
some time in isolation, Clementina asked him to make the introductions
and despite his private misgivings, he accepted.[38] He confided privately to
Lord Pitsligo that he himself suspected that Murray had 'made use of him
as the cat's foot [sic]', with a view to discrediting him in the Jacobite court.[39]
Not long after this, Cardinal Aquaviva consulted with Murray while planning a dinner party concerning the guest list initially planning for twenty
of the king's senior followers to attend. Murray replied that 'the four Irish
gentlemen' (Wogan, Gaydon, O'Toole and Misset) would be fit to attend
and no one else, with the result that only the members of Clementina's
rescue party were invited. This could only have further opened Wogan and
his companions to the resentment and contempt of the Jacobite court. It
would seem that Murray, unable to reconcile the growing tide of anger and
complaints against him in the Jacobite court with the prestige and favour
accorded to Wogan, endeavoured to undermine him.

In recognition of his central role in the planning and accomplishment
of Clementina's rescue and escape from Innsbruck, Wogan was given some
of the most significant marks of honour and prestige possible by the Roman
and Papal authorities. Pope Clement XI conferred the rank of Senator of
Rome upon Wogan and his companions on 15 June 1719. Initially it was
to be just Wogan who would be honoured, but he requested that since his
compatriots had shared an equal portion of the danger, they too should
receive the honour alongside him. The diploma itself, a microfilm copy of

36   Murray stood in for James III's at a proxy marriage ceremony in Bologna in May
     1719 which legally made Clementina James III's wife. Murray performed this task
     because James III was still in Spain.
37   *The Narrative of Lord Pitsligo*, quoted in Tayler, *The Jacobite Court at Rome, 1719*,
     Part I, 54–55.
38   *The Narrative of Lord Pitsligo*, quoted in Tayler, *The Jacobite Court at Rome, 1719*,
     Part I, 61.
39   Ibid.

which is held at the National Library of Ireland, articulates in glowing
and ornate language Wogan's achievement, the first Irishman upon whom
the honour was bestowed.[40] Normally reserved for kings, relatives of the
pope or the Roman nobility, the honour was bestowed on the Irishmen by
Monsignor Francesco Bianchini, Papal Penitentiary, and Count Ippolito
Albani, at a public assembly of Roman nobility, patricians, and citizens on
the Capitol. 'The music of ancient Roman military instruments *(litui and
tubae)* ... accompanied the huge crowd of people in the procession.'[41] The
title allowed those who held it to be addressed as 'Your Excellency'. On
top of this historic bestowal, Monsignior Bianchini organised a *Te Deum*
in honour of Wogan which was to be held at the Basilica of Santa Maria
Maggiore. A letter from Bianchini to James III the day after the Senatorial
honours were bestowed on the Irishmen stated that:

> the four gentlemen who partook in the mission are to be honoured for their great
> success as the Chapter [of the Basilica] of Santa Maria Maggiore propose to cele-
> brate a Te Deum to which Your Majesty and her Serene Highness [the king & Maria
> Clementina] are to be invited with Wogan and his officers in Dillon's regimental
> uniform, and Madame Misset.[42]

Augmenting the high honour of being made Senators of Rome, the five
Irishmen were to receive further public honours in the presence of their
king (not yet returned from Spain) and queen for all to see. They were to
wear the uniforms of Arthur Dillon's Regiment giving public acknow-
ledgement to the role and position of the Irishmen who played their vital
part in the liberation and safe conduct of Clementina to Rome. While
there were probably other occasions when Irish exiles were honoured by
their host societies on the continent during the eighteenth century, such
noteworthy acknowledgements and such a level of ceremony and celebra-
tion was a rare and significant thing. One wonders if news spread about

---

40 British Museum, Add. MS No. 19, 846, N.L.I., n. 785, p. 511.
41 Winch, *The rescue*, 145.
42 The author is grateful to Dr Declan Downey who invited me to accompany him
    on a visit to the Archivio Segreto Vaticano. Francesco Bianchini to James III, 16
    June 1719, Archivio Segreto Vaticano, Segretaria di Stato, Inghilterra, 1700–1745,
    21, 123–126.

the exploits of the rescue party, and the high honours bestowed on them
in Rome, and if it boosted the spirits of the tens of thousands of Irish
exiles living throughout Europe.

Figure 4.1: Regimental Banner of Arthur Dillon's Irish Regiment in France

This image shows the fragment of a flag of Dillon's Regiment, a battlefield standard under which thousands of Irishmen fought in the service of the Kings of France from 1690 to 1789 (Courtesy of the National
Museum of Ireland). The centre of the banner is occupied by a crowned golden harp over a red cross of St
George on a black and red background. It symbolises the Stuart dynasty and their recognition as the only legitimate monarchs of England, Scotland, Wales and Ireland. The Latin words *In Hoc Signo Vinces* translate
as *In this Sign you will Conquer*, an ancient motto of the early Christian church which aligned the regiment
with the Catholic Church. The flag depicted was (according to Dillon family legend) carried during the
Battle of Fontenoy in 1745.

Meanwhile, circumstances at the Jacobite court had deteriorated
significantly. James Murray had been left the task of administering the
court in exile as James III's acting secretary of state in the absence of the
Earl of Mar. His awareness of his precarious position is evident in his
own defensively phrased correspondence with King James while he was in

Spain.[43] Murray seems to have been very overbearing. He was known for over-assuming authority, hoarding responsibility, and of misrepresenting members of the court in his correspondence with King James.[44] His initial botched handling of the introductions was then compounded when he was accused by a circle of high-ranking courtiers of opening and reading the king's correspondence without license.[45] His mentor and predecessor, the Earl of Mar, had quarrelled with him and found him to have lied publicly about their interactions. After Mar had departed from the court again, Lady Mar criticised Murray over his handling of introductions to Queen Clementina and for traducing her poorly at the Jacobite court. Indeed Murray had fostered suspicions about her loyalty in his correspondence with King James.[46] In the end it was Wogan who kept the peace between Lady Mar and Murray at the Jacobite court in June 1719.

The King's Disposition

James had left Italy to travel to Spain in February 1719. James Butler, 2nd Duke of Ormond, had been instrumental in laying the arrangements there for a restoration attempt which would see James restored to his ancestral thrones with Spanish military assistance. The exiled monarch was given a full state welcome to Madrid on 27 March as a guest of high honour by Philip V. The plan had been for an expeditionary force to set sail from Cadiz, pick up James at La Corunna and sail from there to Britain.[47] From the outset, members of his court had been sending him

43   James Murray to James III, Rome, 5 June 1719, quoted in Tayler, *The Jacobite court at Rome, 1719, Part II*, 168–169.

44   Captain John Ogilvie labelled Murray 'a young, vain, white-livered Jackanapes', see Tayler, *The Jacobite court at Rome*, 22.

45   Tayler, *The Jacobite court at Rome, Part I*, 39.

46   James Murray to James III, Rome, 5 June 1719, quoted in Tayler, *The Jacobite court at Rome, 1719, Part II*, 168–169.

47   Corp, *The Jacobite court at Urbino*, 128–135.

letters complaining about each other for various reasons. The constant squabbling among his supporters was a fact of life for James and must have been very irritating. He arrived in La Corunna and was told the crushing news that the incoming Spanish fleet had been weather-blasted, partially wrecked and was unable to sail to Britain. He and his companion John Hay, Earl of Inverness, were forced to stay at Lugo for a tedious three-month waiting period to see if the expedition could be revived or if his supporters would have any success in Scotland. John Hay was a close associate of James Murray and his brother in law through his marriage with Lady Marjory Hay (neé Murray). Hay and Murray had established a powerful and resilient hold over James III during their time at Urbino and had come to prevail over him in many areas. Correspondence from Rome of the constant bickering, accusations against Murray (and made by him), and defensive letters begging the king's understanding would all have been tempered by the comments and observations of John Hay who was at the king's side. Despite the good news of Wogan's rescue of Clementina, the prospect of a lengthy exile in Rome and the undoubted glee of his enemies probably brought James's spirits low indeed. By the time they left Spain for Rome in August 1719, after yet another military disaster, he was most likely in no mood to suffer the tit-for-tat thrusts and ripostes of his followers.

After months of rising tensions at the court, the king was finally re-turning. Murray, hoping to shield himself from criticism, wrote to James on 28 August stating that Clementina had been 'treated with great indif-ference' by the court.[48] This had not been the case and the letter clearly shows Murray's will to misrepresent events to King James. By that stage Lord Pitsligo had had enough of Murray and had already sent a very long letter complaining about Murray which was *en route* to James. In the mean-time, the king sent a letter to Wogan in which he chastised his court for their ill-treatment of Clementina which apparently wasn't shown publicly. Perhaps Wogan, having a fuller picture of the reality of the situation, did not wish to create more chaos and ill-feeling at the court. It appears that

---

48   James Murray to James III, Rome, 5 June 1719, in *The Jacobite court at Rome, Part II*, 175.

James learned of Wogan's attempt at prudence and had a copy of the letter sent to his companion Major Gaydon in Rome. The major did not show the same discretion and he shared the letter (and the king's displeasure) with the court. The question as to why James might have insisted on sending this scolding letter to both Irishmen is an interesting one. Perhaps, knowing his court was congested with followers and dependents, he had hoped they would give him cause to reprimand and remove them if they decried the king's message publicly? Regardless, a copy Lord Pitsligo made of his long, aggrieved letter was finally delivered into James's hands and the king was furious. He sent Pitsligo a crushing reply and held Murray's account of events to be completely true and accurate, utterly dismissing the loyal and well-respected Scottish lord as acting out of jealousy and dishonour. Pitsligo was ordered to leave Rome and quietly returned to Scotland where he wrote his memoire of the events.[49]

A Feather in His Cap

Having examined Wogan's conduct in the years preceding the rescue of Clementina and his navigation of the choppy waters of the court in exile in Rome immediately afterwards, a discussion of James III's choice of how to honour Wogan is worthwhile. The day after the official royal marriage of James Stuart III and Maria Clementina Sobieska at Montefiascone, James created Wogan a Knight-Baronet. While the royal patent itself expresses James' gratitude in warm terms to Wogan, the title is the lowest rank in the British nobiliary system.[50] Indeed, it was invented by James I & IV to raise revenue from the socially ambitious squirearchy and merchant class. The title did not match the significance of the strategic service rendered by Wogan and it contrasts very sharply

---

49   *The Narrative of Lord Pitsligo*, quoted in Tayler, *The Jacobite court in Rome, Part I*, 37. Pitsligo was later vindicated.
50   N.L.I., MS 8340.

with the Roman Senatorship offered by the pope. A letter between the
Earl of Mar and John Hay dated Paris, 19 April 1722 reveals much about
Wogan's honouring:

> ... it was natural to believe that Clementina would have a favourable ear for Wogan
> and Lady Misset who had so eminently assisted her and brought her out of her dif-
> ficulties, and the more because she thought (as I know she did) that they had been
> sacrificed upon her account to Murray and his sister's jealousy and resentment for
> her having looked favourably on them.[51]

Jealous of his achievement, his good relations with the queen and the
honours paid to Wogan, the likelihood is that Murray used his close position with the king to negatively influence James' opinion of Wogan.

Exile within Exile

The reference to having Wogan provided for elsewhere refers to James
III providing brevets of military advancement in a Catholic power of
his choosing for both he and his companions who liberated Clementina.
After a string of military and diplomatic setbacks, Wogan had given
his liege and the Jacobite cause in general a massive strategic, financial
and propagandistic boost. Furthermore, the actions of he and his rescue
party secured the promise of a Stuart successor. Naturally one would
assume that an astute monarch with aspirations such as James III would
do everything in his power to keep his dynamic and competent servants
near him, but in this case the Old Pretender did not. By December 1720
James had to dismiss Murray amidst sustained complaints. In response,
Murray suggested he be given a title to save his reputation before listing
his skills and strengths. In the same letter, he downplayed the role played

---

51   Mar to John Hay, Paris, 19 April 1722, quoted in Tayler, *The Jacobite court in Rome,*
      1719, Part II, 210–214.

by Wogan in the selection of Clementina as his potential bride.[52] James created Murray titular Earl of Dunbar in 1724 and backdated the promotion to February 1721.

Wogan left Italy in December 1719 and was welcomed into the service of Philip V of Spain on his first audience. He joined the Irish Regiment of Limerick and later transferred to the Regimiento d'Irlanda. He wrote to the king in December 1720 asking for a position at James' court and had been denied.[53] In 1721–1722 he returned to Rome to assist Queen Clementina in her struggle to obtain control of her own royal household, but was eventually ordered by James III to leave Rome. He wrote from Madrid in December 1722 asking James to dismiss representations that had been made against him by others about his conduct in Italy and in Spain.[54] Clearly he had enemies at the court who were trying to discredit him there and who must have been somewhat successful. Later, as his exile dragged on, Wogan would confide in Swift[55] that:

> Great and surprising actions, done by a private man, though they may have a momentary glare at their first appearance, never fail of being attested with more envy, than acclamation in the inmost recesses of all hearts. But, among the narrow and lower geniuses, those impressions are either wiped off, or in great measure defaced by the secret intervention of malice. It gives them pain that any man but such as they are bound to admire should execute things, which they, in their own conscience, hold themselves incapable in all other cases.

He consoled himself by citing historical examples of when capable and ingenuitive men were undermined by lesser comrades, and then associated his own experience with that of Scipio Africanus, the Roman General who ended the Punic Wars:

52　Murray to James III, Rome, n.d., December 1720, quoted in Tayler, *The Jacobite court at Rome, 1719, Part II*, 201.

53　Hugh Law, 'Sir Charles Wogan', in *The Journal of the Royal Society of Antiquaries of Ireland*, Seventh Series, Vol., 7, No. 2 (31 December 1937), 259; see also Tayler, *Jacobite epilogue*, 285.

54　Patrick Fagan, ed., *Ireland in the Stuart Papers, 1719–1765*, 2 vols, vol. 1, *1719–1742*, (Dublin, 1995), 36–38.

55　For further discussion of Wogan's correspondence with Swift and of his view of the experience of Irish exiles in Europe, see chapter 1.

in the final words of Scipio the African in the Roman Senate, when the sentence of banishment was read to him, 'Let us ascend the temple of Jupiter, and give thanks to the Gods, this is the anniversary of that day, on which I gained the victory of Zama.'[56]

Even though he felt wronged at what had befallen him at the Stuart court, he was proud of what he had done. He continued to hope for a return to his home in Rathcoffey[57] County Kildare, but it was not to be. When in 1745 the Jacobite insurrection led by Prince Charles Edward gained strength, Wogan lobbied strenuously at the Spanish and French courts to send Irish soldiers, arms and ammunition, but it came to nought. The final challenge for a Stuart restoration ended at Culloden in April 1746. In his later years when he corresponded with Baron Richard Warren[58] he wrote nostalgically of his youth on his ancestral lands in Ireland and signed himself 'Racoffy'.[59] After slow advancement over many years in the Spanish military and successful promotions to the governorship firstly of the province of La Mancha and later to the governorship of Barcelona, Sir Charles Wogan, senator of Rome, died in Spain on 21 July 1754.[60]

56   *The Wogan manuscript*, 20.
57   The author is grateful to Ms Pearl Cosgrave who accompanied him on a visit to Rathcoffey to the ruined medieval castle which belonged to the Wogan family. Ms Cosgrave also confirmed that local people there pronounce the place name omitting the 'th' as silent, as pronounced in the original Gaelic. This is consistent with how Charles Wogan spelled the place name in his writings as 'Racoffy' in his correspondence. See George A. Little 'An Outline for a Life of Warren of Corduff (Part II)', in *Dublin Historical Record*, December, 1968, Vol. 22, No. 4, 301.
58   Baron Warren played a vital role in assisting Prince Charles Edwards escape from Scotland to France after the failure of 'the Forty-five'. His family owned lands in Corduff in North Dublin.
59   Ibid.
60   For a detailed appraisal of Wogan's career in Spain see Richard K. Maher, 'Integration, Identification, and Isolation: a comparative study of the respective experiences of two Irish Jacobites in the court of Philip V', in Igor Perez Tostado & Declan M. Downey, eds, *Ireland and the Iberian Atlantic: migration, military and material culture*, (Valencia, 2020), 287–300.

Bibliography

Primary Sources

Archivio Segreto Vaticano, Segretaria di Stato, Inghilterra, 1700–1745, 21.

British Museum, Add. MS No. 19, 846, N.L.I., n.785, p511.

Calendar of Stuart Papers Volume II, (Historical Manuscripts Commission), (London, 1904).

Galway, Kilmacduagh & Kilfenora Diocesan Archives, *The Wogan manuscript.*

Harris Library, Preston, Community History Pamphlet Collection, Item Number LE75 LET, Anonymous, '*A Letter about the occurrences in the way to, and at Preston, by a gentleman who was an eyewitness to the said transactions*'.

National Library of Ireland, MS 8340.

Secondary Sources

Anonymous, *The secret history of the rebels in Newgate*, (London, 1717).

Carroll, Clare Lois, *Exiles in a global city: the Irish in Early Modern Rome, 1609–1783*, (Leiden, 2018).

Corp, Edward, *The Jacobites at Urbino, an exiled court in transition*, (New York, 2008).

D'Arcy, Frank, 'Exiles and strangers: the case of the Wogans', in O'Brien, Gerard, (Ed.), *Parliament, politics and people; essays in eighteenth-century Irish history*, (Dublin, 1989).

Defoe, Daniel, *The history of the Press Yard: ...*, (London 1717).

Fagan, Patrick, ed., *Ireland in the Stuart Papers, 1719–1765*, 2 vols, vol. 1, *1719–1742*, (Dublin, 1995).

Hayes, R., *Irish swordsmen of France*, (Dublin, 1934).

Law, Hugh, 'Sir Charles Wogan', in *The Journal of the Royal Society of Antiquaries of Ireland*, Seventh Series, Vol. 7, No. 2, (31 December 1937).

Little, George A., 'An outline for a life of Warren of Corduff (Part II)', in *Dublin Historical Record*, Vol. 22, No. 4, (December, 1968).

Maher, Richard K., 'Integration, identification, and isolation: a comparative study of the respective experiences of two Irish Jacobites in the court of Philip V', in Recio Morales, Oscar and Perez Tostado, Igor, eds, *Proceedings of the second international congress on Ireland and Iberian Atlantic, Cuartel General de la Fuerza Terrestre (Capitania General), Seville, 27 & 28 October 2016*, (Seville, 2020).

Maher, Richard K., *'No good deed goes unpunished': Charles Wogan and his Removal from the Jacobite court in Rome, June 1719*', (M.A. Thesis, University College Dublin, 2013, unpublished).

Maher, Richard K., 'Poems from the prison yard; poetic correspondence between Charles Wogan and William Tunstall', in *History Ireland*, Vol. 25, No. 2, (March/April 2017).

O'Kelly de Galway, Alphonse, *Mémoire Historique et Généalogique sur la Famille de Wogan*, (Paris, 1896).

Patten, Robert, *The history of the rebellion in the year 1715: with original papers, and the characters of the principal noblemen and gentlemen concern'd in it*, (London, 1717).

Szechi, Daniel, *1715, the Great Jacobite Rebellion*, (Bury, 2006).

Tayler, Henrietta, *The Jacobite court at Rome, 1719*. Publications of the Scottish Historical Society, Third Series, Volume XXXI. (Edinburgh, 1938).

Tayler, Henrietta, *Jacobite epilogue: a further selection of letters from Jacobites among the Stuart papers at Windsor published by the gracious permission of his Majesty the King*, (London, 1941).

Wills, Rebecca, *The Jacobites and Russia, 1715–50*, (Dundern, 2002).

Winch, Cathy, *The rescue of Clementina Stuart*, (Belfast, 2008).

DECLAN M. DOWNEY

5 The Habsburg-Hanoverian Alliance and Its perspective on the Stuart-Sobieska match

Introduction

The rescue of Maria Clementina Sobieska (1701–1735) from Innsbrück by a group of daring Irish adherents of the exiled Stuart claimant to the thrones of England, Scotland and Ireland; James III & VIII (1701–1766); and her subsequent marriage to him at Montefiascone near Rome has provided much material for Jacobite propaganda, romanticism and nostalgia. This historic episode with its undeniably dramatic details of swashbuckling derring-do has at its core two traditional villains, His Britannic Majesty and prince-elector of Hanover,[1] George I (1714–1727), and His Apostolic Imperial Majesty, Charles VI (1711–1740). Given the former's identification with the continuity of the 'usurpation' of the legitimate rights of the Catholic king, James II & VII (1685–1701), in 1688 and of his son and heir, James III & VIII, and with the preservation of the Whig and Protestant (Anglican) Interest in Britain and Ireland under the Hanoverian Succession (1711–1837), it is baffling for those who are

---

1 'Hanover' is the anglicised form of Hannover, the capital of the Prince-Electorate of Braunschweig-Lüneburg. For ease and simplicity, the English found it convenient to substitute the anglicised form of the capital's name for the official name of the state, as they simultaneously anglicised Braunschweig to 'Brunswick'.

imbued in religious and political Manichaeism, and for those who are
unfamiliar with the political and diplomatic details, intricacies and nu-
ances of the equilibrium among the European Powers since the Peace of
Westphalia (1648), to understand why the foremost Catholic monarch of
the age, the Holy Roman Emperor of the German Nation, should support the ostensible enemies of his religion, never mind the usurpation of
his fellow Catholic monarch. This essay will attempt an exploration of
the origins and nature of the Anglo-Hanoverian-Austrian Habsburg and
Imperial alliances and relations within contemporary European power-
equilibrium politics. Also, it will endeavour to explain the confluence
of interests between this combination and those of the French regent,
Philippe II Duc d'Orléans regarding Swedish as well as Spanish Bourbon
ambitions and dealings with the exiled Stuart court in the period 1700
to 1719.

Divergent Cultures of Tolerance

While early modern French statecraft as exemplified by Louis XI,
François I, Henri IV, Cardinal Richelieu and Cardinal Mazarin is ac-
credited generally with the de-confessionalisation or secularisation of
politics and diplomacy,[2] it should not be forgotten that in the Imperial
Germanic sphere, politico-religious concord and ecumenical collaboration between Catholics and Lutherans had been enunciated as early as
1555 in the Peace of Augsburg, and subsequently it extended to include
Calvinists in the Peace of Westphalia in 1648. It was the latter settlement
which consisted of two international treaties signed at Osnabrück and
at Münster that established the concept of the Balance of Power and its

2   Francois Hildesheimer, *Richelieu, une certaine idée de* l'état, (Paris, 1985); Victor-
     Lucien Tapié, *La politique étrangère de la France et le début de la Guerre de Trente
     Ans (1616–1621)*, (Paris 1934); Joseph Bergin, *The rise of Richelieu*, (Yale 1991, repr.
     Manchester & New York, 1997); Pierre Goubert, *Mazarin*, (Paris, 1990), Geoffrey
     Treasure, *Mazarin: The Crisis of Absolutism in France*, (London, 1995).

practice in the conduct of International Relations right up to the present. The experience of the horrors unleased by fundamentalist bigotry and opportunist greed during the Thirty Years War (1618–1648) convinced the intelligent that Christianity was far too important to be allowed to become the sole preserve of fundamentalists, puritans and *holier-than-thou* types. Within the Holy Roman Empire of the German Nation, the Catholic, Lutheran and Calvinist denominations were represented equally in the *Corpus Catholicorum* and the *Corpus Evangelicorum* in the *Reichstag*, and their liberties and privileges were guaranteed by the imperial constitution, the legal code and by the *Kaiser* himself.[3] Even in the small prince-electorate of Braunschweig-Lüneburg religious tolerance for its Lutherans, Catholics and the Calvinist minority was the norm, legally and culturally. Even its ruling dynasty, the House of Welf, had Lutheran and Catholic branches.[4] It is not generally known that as early as April 1718, George I had wanted to introduce bills to the British parliament for religious toleration and social justice for Roman Catholics, Dissenters (Presbyterians, Baptists, Quakers) and Jews, he and James Stanhope, First Lord of the Treasury and Chancellor of the Exchequer, and John Churchill, Duke of Marlborough and President of the Council, were forced to withdraw the bill amid a barrage of parliamentarian insults aimed at their new German-born and bred king.[5] In this context, it is worth remembering how the Irish parliament had caused similar embarrassment to William III in 1692 and 1697 when to his dismay and that of his Catholic allies such as Emperor Leopold I, it refused to ratify the *Articles of Limerick* and proceeded to pass a series of penal laws to restrict Catholicism in Ireland, most notoriously the Popery Act of 1704.[6]

3   Karl Otmar von Aretin. *Das Reich: Friedensgarantie und europäisches Gleichgewicht 1648–1806*, (Stuttgart, 1986).

4   Franz Wilhelm Woker, *Geschichte der Katholischen Kirche und Gemeinde in Hannover und Celle*, (Paderborn, 1889); Thomas Scharf-Wrede, ed., *Katholisch in Hannover; Menschen-Geschichten-Lebenswelten. Quellen und Studien zur Geschichte und Kunst in Bistum Hildesheim*, 11, (Hildesheim, 2019).

5   Ragnhild Hatton, *George I. Elector and King*, (London, 1978), 202–203.

6   John Gerald Simms, *The Williamite confiscation in Ireland, 1690–1703*, (London, 1956), 55–65; Idem, *Jacobite Ireland, 1685–91*, (London, 1969, repr. Dublin, 2000), 258–265; Charles Ivar McGrath, 'Securing the protestant interest: the origins

Hanoverian Strategic Dependence on its Austrian and Imperial Alliances

Braunschweig-Lüneburg or Hanover as it is more commonly known in English, was a small north German state that was almost surrounded by the larger and more powerful Hohenzollern dynastic possessions of Brandenburg-Prussia to the east and Jülich-Kleef to the west, and by the Dutch Republic to the north-west, and by the prince-bishopric of Münster and the Landgraviate of Hesse to the south. It had, under its successive electoral princes, Ernst-August and George I, aligned itself closely with the Austrian Habsburg dynasty for protection in the political and strategic affairs of the Holy Roman Empire. Imperial protection which was dependent on Austrian economic, military and political strength, ensured Hanover's survival as an autonomous principality.[7] This became particularly apparent during Louis XIV's belligerent attempts to dominate Europe which were opposed by the Imperial-Anglo-Dutch alliance in the War of the League of Augsburg (1688–1697). This conflict included the 'War of the Two Kings'[8] in Ireland (1688–1691), whereby James II & VII lost England, Scotland and Ireland to William III, and subsequently set the Hanoverian Succession in motion. Furthermore, electoral status enhanced the prestige of the Welf dynasty as it was ranked immediately below the office of emperor and gave it pre-eminence over other princes and princelings in the empire.[9]

---

and purpose of the penal laws of 1695', in *Irish Historical Studies*, Vol. 30, No. 117, (May, 1996), 25–46.

7   *Hannover Hauptstaatsarchiv, iii Calenberg Brief Archiv*, II EI, nos. 99, 177, 258 provide excellent primary source information concerning George I's relations with the Holy Roman Emperor Charles VI and the Empire.

8   'Cogadh an Dá Rí ' or 'War of the two kings', also called 'The Williamite War', see Éamonn Ó Ciardha, *Ireland and the Jacobite Cause, 1685–1766*, (Dublin, 2002), 52; William Maguire, ed., *Kings in conflict: the revolutionary war in Ireland 1688–91*, (Belfast, 1990), 2.

9   Hatton, *George I*, 30–64.

Personal Bonds and Familial Ties

Further expression of the strength of the almost symbiotic relationship between the Houses of Braunschweig and Habsburg may be noted in George's
participation with his brother Frederick in the Imperial and Polish forces
led by Prince Eugene of Savoy and King Jan Sobieski in the repulsion of the
Ottoman Turks from the gates of Vienna on 12 September 1683.[10] On the
death of his father in 1692, George's succession as prince-elector was recognised by Emperor Leopold I who later confirmed George's title and conferred
on him the position of Arch-Bannerer of the Holy Roman Empire on 23
January 1698. In 1701, under the terms of Britain and Ireland's parliamentary Act of Settlement, George, through his mother Sophia (granddaughter
of James I & VI), became heir designate to the throne, with his imperial
overlord's assent.[11] On the outbreak of the War of the Spanish Succession
(1700–1715), George rallied to the colours of Archduke Charles of Austria,
Leopold's younger son, who claimed the Spanish throne on the death of its
last Habsburg king, Charles II, in opposition to Philippe d'Anjou, grandson
of Louis XIV of France. In 1707, George was appointed field marshal and
commander of the Imperial army of the Rhine in the allied Anglo-Dutch-
Imperial forces (almost a continuation of the previous League of Augsburg),
under the joint leadership of the aforementioned Duke of Marlborough
and Prince Eugene of Savoy.[12] In 1710, George was elevated to the dignity of
Arch-Treasurer of the Holy Roman Empire.[13] In the following year, Emperor
Joseph I died unexpectedly, and his younger brother, Archduke Charles,
who had claimed the Spanish throne in 1700, and resided in Barcelona from
1705 onwards, and was married to George's cousin, Elisabeth Christine of
Braunschweig-Wolfenbüttel in 1708,[14] succeeded to the Imperial throne. This
changed the war aims and foreign policy objectives of Britain and the Dutch

---

10   Hatton, *George I*, 43, 49, 84, 85.
11   Hatton, *George I*, 30–64, 78–110.
12   Hatton, *George I*, 88, 89, 100–104, 132, 133, 173.
13   Hatton, *George I*, 15.
14   Hatton, *George I*, 63, 126; Frank Huss, *Der Wiener Kaiserhof. Eine Kulturgeschichte von Leopold I. bis Leopold II*, (Gernsbach, 2008), 85–90.

Republic. Neither wanted to see the emergence of a Bourbon dynastic mono-
lith combining France and Spain and their respective overseas possessions, as
it would disturb the international Balance of Power. Yet, London and The
Hague were equally unenthusiastic about the prospect of the revival of the
Reichsidée und Reichsmacht of Emperor Charles V (1519–1555) in the dynastic
reunification of Austrian-Spanish-Burgundian Netherlandish and German
Imperial resources. Such a monolithic power would be considered even more
intimidating than a Franco-Spanish dynastic union. Thus, relations between
Vienna and her allies in London and The Hague became strained, though the
friendship between George and Charles remained strong.[15]

Following the death of William III in 1702, and the accession of
Queen Anne, both Sidney Godolphin, Earl of Godolphin and Lord High
Treasurer, and Marlborough were foremost in maintaining Britain's par-
ticipation in the Anglo-Dutch-Austrian-Imperial alliance as an insurance
or security against Louis XIV's ambitions and the ever-present menace of
the Stuart claimant, James III & VIII, and the Jacobite card being played.
Yet such policies could only be maintained at great expense among in-
creasingly war weary taxpayers.[16] Soon, another re-emergence of periodic
Anglo-insularism found expression among the High Tories who felt that
Britain's military and naval capabilities as well as her strategic and commercial interests were being sacrificed in the interests of the Dutch, the
Austrians and their continental allies. This mood coincided with the loss
of influence that Godolphin, Marlborough and his lady-wife, Sarah, had
with Queen Anne, and their replacement in 1711 by Sarah's first cousin,
Abigail Masham as Keeper of the Privy Purse and her cousin, Robert
Harley as Lord High Treasurer and raised to the peerage as Earl of Oxford
and Mortimer, and Henry St John, Viscount Bolingbroke as Secretary of
State.[17] Both Oxford and Bolingbroke moved swiftly to resolve the dismal
economic financial situation by reducing revenues to sustain Marlborough's
military commitments on the continent, and by upgrading their secret negotiations with the French into which they had entered as early as October

15   Brendan Simms, *Three victories and a defeat: the rise and fall of the first British
      Empire, 1714–1783*, (London, 2007), 118, 159, 167–168, 172–173.
16   Basil Williams, *Stanhope. A study in eighteenth-century war and diplomacy*,
      (Oxford, 1932, repr. 1968), 44, 53, 58, 62, 65, 73–74, 80, 87, 99, 135, 256, 266.
17   Clayton Roberts, 'The fall of the Godolphin Ministry', in *Journal of British
      Studies*, Vol. 22, No. 1 (autumn 1982), 71–93.

1710. This occurred just before the future British statesman and key-player in countering Jacobite intrigues, James Stanhope, then a general in joint-command with Marshal Count Guido von Starhemberg of the allied Anglo-Habsburg forces, was taken captive by Marshal Louis-Joseph de Bourbon, Duc de Vendôme after the surrender of Brihuega in Castilla-La Mancha on 9 December 1710.[18]

Figure 5.1: Holy Roman Emperor Charles VI

Ján Kupecký, *Kaiser Karl VI [Emperor Charles VI]*, 1716, no measurements available, oil on canvas (Courtesy of the Vienna Museum). This portrait of Charles shows the emperor in his prime. The dark background provides vivid contrast with the monarch's face and rich attire.

18 Williams, *Stanhope*, 106–115, 117, 121–125.

A Periodic Anglo-Insularist Reversal

Meanwhile, on 17 April 1711, Emperor Joseph I died, and his brother, Charles who had returned to Vienna from Barcelona was elected to the Imperial dignity on 12 October that year. This in itself was a game-changer as it was used as a justification for the *Preliminary Articles of Peace* which Harley and Jean-Baptiste Colbert de Torcy, Louis XIV's foreign minister, had signed four days earlier on 8 October. According to the *Preliminary Articles* Philippe d'Anjou would retain the Spanish Crown and her possessions in the Americas, the Caribbean, the Pacific and in Africa as Philip V of Spain, while Charles of Austria would be compensated with the former Spanish Netherlands and territories in the Italian Peninsula and recognised as Holy Roman Emperor. In return, Britain would receive strategic and commercial advantages in trade with France and Spain and the monopoly on the trans-Atlantic slave trade.[19]

The clandestine Anglo-French negotiations did not escape the attention of the Imperial ambassador to Britain, Count Johann Wenzel von Gallas. He kept Vienna informed on a frequent basis and he proposed that a visit by Prince Eugene – regarded as a hero by many in Britain at that time – might help thwart the emerging Anglo-French amity and restore Marlborough to queenly favour. However, Gallas was unaware that his communications in cypher had been betrayed to Bolingbroke who advised the queen to refuse Gallas reception at Court.[20] Indeed, Bolingbroke's instructions to the British ambassador in The Hague at that time have quite a remarkable resonance today with the current Tory government's attitude and policy towards the European Union:

> Your excellency is to discourage as much as possible, this prince [Eugene] coming over. It is high time to put a stop to this foreign influence on British councils; and we must either emancipate ourselves now or be forever slaves.[21]

19   Brian W. Hill, 'Oxford, Bolingbroke, and the peace of Utrecht', in *The Historical Journal*, Vol. 16, No. 2, (June 1973), 241–263.
20   Nicholas Henderson, *Prince Eugene of Savoy. A biography*, (London, 1964, repr. 2002), 185–189.
21   Bolingbroke to Ambassador Thomas Wentworth, third earl of Strafford, quoted in Gilbert Parke, ed., *Letters and correspondence of Henry St John, Lord Viscount Bolingbroke*, 4 vols, (London, 1798), II, 52.

Even though Eugene visited London between January and March 1712, Marlborough had by then been dismissed from all his offices, and Jonathan Swift's pamphlet, *The Conduct of Allies*, published in the previous November and which had sold over 11,000 copies, had succeeded in its purpose of whipping-up a populist frenzy in favour of the government's peace initiative with France. Not only was Charles VI infuriated at the Anglo-French Preliminary Articles of Peace, but so also were the Dutch who now felt that the Anglo-Dutch Barrier Treaty of 1709 was worthless and that they had been betrayed to the French. Unsurprisingly, Marlborough as well as the Whig Party which was then dominant in the House of Lords opposed Harley and Bolingbroke's conciliation with France. However, it was not without significance that the heir designate to the British throne, George of Hanover, condemned the Anglo-French machinations as a betrayal of the Austrian and Imperial alliance.[22]

Equilibrium Renewed

On 1 August 1714, Queen Anne died, and her Hanoverian cousin was crowned as George I in Westminster Abbey on 20 October that year. Marlborough returned to Court at the king's request, Harley and Bolingbroke fell from power and favour while the Whigs returned to power under James Montagu Earl of Halifax, Sir Robert Walpole, Charles Townshend and the aforementioned James Stanhope.[23] Though in failing health, Marlborough and his protégé and former Chief of Staff, William Cadogan of Liscarton County Meath directed operations in the suppression of the Jacobite Uprising in Scotland in 1715.[24] A year later, Louis XIV died on 9 September, and was succeeded by his great-grandson the 5-year-old Louis XV, but power was exercised by Philippe II, Duc d'Orléans,

22   Hatton, *George I*, 104–107.
23   Williams, *Stanhope*, 121–168.
24   Daniel Szechi, *1715: the Great Jacobite rebellion*, (Yale, 2006), 164–167.

nephew of the late Sun-King. The regent's mother, Elisabeth-Charlotte la Madame Palatine, was a niece of Sophia of Hanover (to whom she was very close) and first cousin of George I.[25] Her daughter, Elisabeth-Charlotte la Petite Fille de France, would marry Duke Leopold Joseph of Lorraine et Bar, and their son, Francis Stephen would marry Maria Theresa, daughter and heiress of Charles VI, in 1736.[26] This combination of familial links in conjunction with the new realities of the European balance of power and its concurrent friendlier Anglo-Hanoverian-French-Imperial relations confronted the rival Stuart claimant, James III & VIII.

Between April 1713 and February 1715, a series of treaties were signed between the warring powers became collectively known as the Peace of Utrecht that eventually ended the War of the Spanish Succession. Building upon the earlier Westphalian Peace's equilibrium among the powers, the Peace of Utrecht established the principle in international affairs that in the interests of stability and peace, dynastic rights should neither disturb nor take precedence over the international balance of power. It is in this politico-diplomatic context that The War of the Spanish Succession was ended with the confirmation of the *Preliminary Articles* with some modifications and the new equilibrium and relative stability among the European powers was set for the next thirty-five years until the outbreak of the War of the Austrian Succession.[27] It was in these new circumstances that the aspirations and claims of James Stuart upon the thrones of Britain and Ireland faced immense difficulties, and the Jacobite cause would acquire the status of a mere diversionary tactic on the strategic chessboard of the European powers.[28]

25   Hatton, *George I*, 20, 24–27, 37, 72, 74, 135, 139, 160, 196; Charlotte-Elisabeth de Bavière, Duchesse d'Orléans, *Correspondence complete de Madame duchesse d'Orléans née princesse palatine, mère du régent,* collated and edited by Gustave Brune, 2 vols, (Paris, 1855, 3rd edn 1863).
26   Huss, *Der Wiener Kaiserhof,* 78.
27   Alfred H. A. Soons, ed., *The 1713 peace of Utrecht and its enduring effects.* Nota et Vetera Iuris Gentium Series, (Leiden and Boston, 2019).
28   Daniel Szechi, *The Jacobites. Britain and Europe 1688–1788,* (Manchester and New York, 1994), 85–125.

The Lotharingian Dimension

After the Treaty of Rijswijk in 1697, Louis XIV was compelled by the League of Augsburg to restore the duchy of Lorraine et Bar to its rightful duke, Leopold Joseph, whose mother, Eleanor of Austria, was an aunt of Emperor Charles VI. The duke's mentor and chancellor (chief minister) was Francis Taaffe, earl of Carlingford, who, until his death in 1704, oversaw the restoration of the duchy's economy as well as the ducal foreign policy of steering a friendly course between Vienna and Versailles, and to this end, Taaffe helped arrange the marriage between Duke Leopold and the aforementioned Elizabeth-Charlotte d'Orléans, on 13 October 1698.[29]

In 1713, the Anglo-French Peace negotiated by Oxford and Bolingbroke with Torcy stipulated that the Stuart claimant, James III & VIII and his court in exile would depart from the Kingdom of France. With their connivance, and that of Charles VI, Leopold I, and Eugene of Savoy, James, under the title Chevalier de St-Georges became resident at Bar-le-Duc, part of the sovereign duchy of Lorraine et Bar which was outside the Holy Roman Empire and considered a protectorate of France.[30] While there, the Stuart claimant's half-brother, James FitzJames Duke of Berwick, nephew of Marlborough, commanded the Bourbon forces that seized Barcelona from Habsburg loyalists after a lengthy siege on 11 September 1714 and thereby brought a decisive end to the War of the Spanish Succession.[31] Between March 1714 and March 1715, an interesting correspondence between the half-brothers, indicates that they were aware of strains in Anglo-Austrian-Imperial relations

29 *Österreichische Staatsarchiv Wien, Hofkriegratsprotokoll, 1677, fol.53. HKR an Lothringen, Jänner;* O'Donell, D. *Die Abstammung, Familien und Taten der österreichischen Generäle irisher Herkunft in Siebenjährigen Krieg,* (Universität Wien, Unpublished M.Phil. Thesis, 1998), 145–146.

30 Nathalie Genet-Rouffiac, *Le grand exil: les jacobites en France, 1688–1745,* (Paris, 2007); Frédéric Richard-Maupillier, 'The Irish in the Regiments of Duke Leopold of Lorraine, 1698–1729', in *Archivium Hibernicum,* Vol. 67, (2014), 285–321.

31 Declan M. Downey, 'Beneath the Harp and the Burgundian Cross: Irish regiments in the Spanish Bourbon Army, 1700–1818', in Hugo O'Donnell, ed., *Presencia irlandesa en la milicia española. The Irish presence in the Spanish Military – 16th to 20th centuries,* (Madrid, 2014), especially 88–89; see also 97–101.

over the Anglo-French Peace of 1713, and thus they considered initiatives to establish friendly relations with Charles VI, appoint a diplomatic representative to his court and secure support from him, and they even discussed a marriage alliance with a princess of the House of Habsburg.[32] However, such ideas remained in dreamland, and any hopes of a Jacobite-Habsburg alliance that they may have entertained were soon dashed upon the crags of the failed Jacobite Uprising in Scotland in 1715.

On 4 February 1716, when James returned to France from his disastrous attempt at a restoration in Scotland, his residency in Lorraine et Bar was untenable as Duke Leopold's imperial obligations demanded that he could not provide refuge to one who had assaulted the sovereign rights over Britain of George I, the imperial archchancellor and prince-elector of Hanover. Thus, the Stuart claimant was obliged to remove himself and his court from the duchy to the papal enclave of Avignon in April that year. Later after sojourns at Pesaro and Urbino, the Jacobite Court in exile was given refuge in Rome from November 1718 until James' death in 1766.[33]

George I's Anglo-Austrian Rapprochement

Ever since George I's accession to the British throne, both he and his Whig government had sought to make amends for Oxford and Bolingbroke's machinations with France in 1711–1712, and for the treachery in their

---

32   Berwick to James, 28 March 1714, in Francis Henry Blackburne Daniell, ed., *Historical manuscripts commission, calendar of Stuart Papers*, I, (London, 1902), 311; Berwick to James, 1 January 1715, *H.M.C., Stuart Papers*, I, 340; Berwick to James, 11 January 1715, *H.M.C., Stuart Papers*, I, 343; Berwick to James, 1 March 1715, *H.M.C., Stuart Papers*, I, 350; Berwick to James, 10 March 1715, *H.M.C., Stuart Papers*, 352; James to Berwick, 19 March 1715, *H.M.C., Stuart Papers*, I, 354; An interesting exploratory study regarding the attempts of James III & VIII to initiate diplomatic representation at the Imperial Court may be found in S. J. Griffin, *The Jacobite diplomats to the court of Emperor Charles VI, 1716–1740: a study in eighteenth century diplomacy* (unpublished MA dissertation, University of Limerick, 2016).

33   Edward Corp, *The Stuarts in Italy, 1719–1766: a royal court in permanent exile*, (Cambridge, 2011).

secret instructions to Marlborough's replacement, James Butler, Duke of Ormond, to abandon their Austrian and Dutch allies at the Battle of Denain in 1712.[34] George himself had been almost killed at Prince Eugene's side during that combat, and therefore he had a personal interest in settling that matter and in keeping Britain engaged in continental combinations to balance against the might of France.[35] Herein lies another significant factor in the personal, dynastic and politico-diplomatic and military alliance between George I and Charles VI in our understanding of their mutual interest in keeping such relations alive and healthy. The security of the personal union of Hanover and Britain under George I depended upon the support of alliances with Austria, the Holy Roman Empire and the Dutch Republic, as much as Austria and the Dutch Republic's security depended upon Hanoverian military strength in combination with British naval power. Such strategic considerations were well appreciated by George I and his Whig ministers, Walpole, Townshend and Stanhope, the Hanoverian chancellor, Count Andreas von Bernstorff, Marlborough, Prince Eugene of Savoy and Charles VI. Past experience of the War of the League of Augsburg and the War of the Spanish Succession testified to the importance of such alliances in containing Bourbon ambitions and in maintaining the balance of power. With the onset of new threats to that equilibrium from Sweden, Russia, Spain and the Ottoman Empire, it was in the mutual interests of George I and Charles VI to renew and re-invigorate their relations in the Treaty of Westminster in 25 May–5 June 1716. Within three weeks of the treaty's conclusion, the Irish émigré, Owen O'Rourke, who was grand chamberlain to Duke Leopold of Lorraine et Bar, and a protégé of the duchy's late chancellor, Francis Taaffe, had advised the Stuart claimant's prime minister, the Earl of Mar: 'A man employed by our King will either be not received there [the Imperial Court in Vienna] at all, or kept at such a distance from affairs as might render him very despicable.'[36] Clearly, this

---

34   Henderson, *Prince Eugene*, 180–211; Simms, *Three victories and a defeat*, 66–67, 97–99, 101–125.

35   Simms, *Three victories*, 67.

36   Owen O'Rourke to Earl of Mar, 27 June 1716, *H.M.C., Stuart Papers*, II, (London, 1904), 238.

was a warning that the time was inauspicious for James III & VIII to initiate friendly overtures to Charles VI.

It says much about James III's lack of political awareness or sensitivity as much as it does about Mar's *gaucherie*, that both pressed ahead with the appointment of John Walkingshaw, a merchant and 'wee laird' of Barrowfield, who had escaped after the Uprising of 1715 to Bar-le-Duc. Bereft of serious social status or connections, he was appointed 'to negotiate with the Emperor or his ministers'.[37] Little is known of him and it is doubtful if he even spent time in Vienna, except that by 1717, he seems to have availed of a general pardon from George I and returned to Glasgow to resume his mercantile life and where his youngest daughter, Clementina, was born in 1720.[38] Later, she would become the mistress of Bonnie Prince Charlie.[39]

Swedish and Spanish Intrigues with the Jacobites

By 1717, the Anglo-Hanoverian-Habsburg alliance was on the offensive. Austria was at war with the Ottoman Empire (1716–1718), pushing back the Sultan's renewed onslaught whereby Habsburg rule became extended into Serbia and Lesser Wallachia. Simultaneously, Charles VI had to defend imperial interests and those of Brandenburg-Prussia, Saxony and Hannover against the aggression of King Charles XII of Sweden during the Great Northern War (1700-1721). Another cause for concern among the emperor and the imperial magnates at this time was the continued Russian occupation of Mecklenburg which led them to question the intentions of their ally, Tsar Peter the Great. It was within this context that

---

37 James to Walkingshaw, 6 November 1716.
     H.M.C., Stuart Papers, III, (London, 1907), 192–193.
38 John Guthrie Smith & John Oswald Mitchell, *The old country houses of the old Glasgow gentry,* (Glasgow, 1878), XCIX Wolfe House.
39 Frank McLynn, *Bonnie Prince Charlie,* (London, 1988), 168, 333–344, 349, 355, 366–369, 374.

the duchies of Bremen and Verden (which had been under Swedish control since 1648 until they were lost to King Frederick IV of Denmark in 1712), were subsequently sold to Hanover in October 1715. This transaction, which now gave the Hanoverian Electorate its own territorial access to the sea also brought it into direct conflict with Sweden. Since Britain and Hanover were separate sovereign realms, Stockholm and London did not engage in mutual declarations of war. However, domestic political sensitivities in Britain increased over her resources and interests being compromised by Hanoverian ambitions which caused diplomatic difficulties in Anglo-Swedish relations. [40] Thus, by January 1717, the Swedish ambassadors in Paris, The Hague and London, Baron Erik Sparre, Baron George Görtz von Schlitz and Count Karl Gyllenborg, respectively, initiated intrigues with local Jacobite agents. [41] George needed Charles's help in securing northern Germany against both Sweden and Russia, as well as the emperor's confirmation of the incorporation of Bremen and Verden into George's prince-electorate to comply with the laws and constitution of the Holy Roman Empire. [42]

Meanwhile, Philip V and his queen-consort, Elisabeth Farnese, emboldened by the swift and successful economic recovery of Spain under their astute chief minister, Giulio Cardinal Alberoni, sought to reverse the Peace of Utrecht's exclusion of Philip's right of succession to the French throne (on the basis that it was illegal under French Law), as well as reclaim Italian possessions that had been ceded to Charles VI, and recover the two strategic fortified bases of Port Mahón and Gibraltar that Britain had gained in 1715. [43] In this matter, the ambitions of the French regent, Orléans, to succeed his sickly young cousin, Louis XV, on the throne were threatened, as indeed was the future of France if it were to be drawn by a personal union with Spain under Philip into another costly war against an

40 Paul Samuel Fritz, *The English Ministers and Jacobitism between the rebellions of 1715 and 1745*, (Toronto, 1975), 28–40.

41 J. F. Chance, 'The "Swedish Plot" of 1716–7', in *English Historical Review*, Vol. XVIII, (1903), 81–106; Szechi, *The Jacobites*, 104–107.

42 Hatton, *George I*, 33–39, 166–168, 183–193, 200, 220–224, 230–231, 236–238, 240–243, 269–271, 277–279, 295.

43 Szechi, *The Jacobites*, 107–109.

Anglo-Hanoverian-Dutch-Austrian-Imperial alliance.[44] The situation escalated with the discovery of the 'Cellamare Conspiracy' against Orléans, and the Spanish seizure of Sardinia in 1717 without opposition as Austrian forces were ranged against the Ottoman Turks. Thus, Philip V and Alberoni ordered their forces to invade Sicily in July 1718.

By that stage, both the British secretary, Stanhope and Orléans' close adviser and special agent, the Abbé Guillaume Dubois (created foreign minister in 1720 and Cardinal in 1721), had already met secretly in The Hague in July and in Hanover in August 1617, to agree terms for what would become the Triple Alliance of Britain, France and the Dutch Republic, to confront and contain Bourbon Spain, while simultaneously giving security to Hanover, Brandenburg-Prussia and Denmark in their struggle with Sweden over Schleswig, Holstein and Gottorp, and in their efforts to ensure a Russian withdrawal from Mecklenburg.[45] Meanwhile, Charles VI, though annoyed at his Anglo-Dutch allies for treating with his traditional foe, France, was soon persuaded by Prince Eugene, Stanhope and the prospect of British naval support in the Mediterranean to join them and France in what became known as the Quadruple Alliance.[46] Herein we can see, once again, another instance of the operation of the Balance of Power on the European strategic chessboard.

Thwarted by the Quadruple Alliance, and the devastation of the Spanish fleet off Sicily's Cape Passaro by an Anglo-Dutch squadron under Admiral George Byng's command in August 1718, Philip V and Alberoni played the Jacobite card with the Swedes in opening a new diversion for Britain-Hanover with the Jacobite Uprising of 1719.[47] In March 1719, James III & VIII, left Rome for Madrid where he oversaw preparations for two Jacobite-Spanish expeditions, one bound for England under the

44   Williams, *Stanhope*, 200–229; Szechi, *The Jacobites*, 90–91.

45   *Archives du Ministère des Affaires Étrangères, Paris, Angleterre*, 277, ff. 22–26, ff 20–38, 128–133, 150, 226–227, 274–288; Williams, *Stanhope*, 211–229.

46   Though the Dutch had agreed to the Quadruple Alliance, they did not actually sign the agreement, but Savoy did sign it as its Sicilian territory had been invaded by Spain, see Henry Kamen, *Philip V of Spain. The king who reigned twice*, (Yale, New Haven and London, 2001), 124–125; Williams, *Stanhope*, 253–313.

47   Szechi, *The Jacobites*, 104–111; Kamen, *Philip V*, 107–130.

aforementioned Ormond's command, and the other for Scotland under George Keith, the Earl Marischal. On 29 March, the proverbial 'English Protestant Wind' broke forcing Ormond's great flotilla back to Spain, but Keith's expedition arrived on Scotland's west coast, however, the attempt for a Jacobite restoration there ended at Glenshiel on 10 June 1719, James's thirty-first birthday.[48]

It was against this backdrop of the Quadruple Alliance's confrontation of Bourbon Spain and its Jacobite protégés in 1719, and of the special strategic alliances of Austria and the Holy Roman Empire with Hanover since 1648, of Austria with Britain since 1688, that we can appreciate why Charles VI obliged his proven ally, George I, in detaining Princess Maria Clementina Sobieska at Innsbrück in spring 1719. Quite apart from the obligations of the emperor to his ally, as is evident from the foregoing, there was an amicable personal relationship between Charles and George, reinforced by the latter's cousin, the formidable empress-consort, Elisabeth-Christine *die Wolfenbüttlerin*, as she was known among the Viennese.[49] The prospect of a Sobieska-Stuart marriage alliance and its attendant transfer of immense wealth from the princess' dowry into the hands of the Stuart claimant and the political use to which it might be put, was not lost on either the Anglo-Hanoverian regime nor the *Reichshofrat* and most notably, Prince Eugene. In addition to the dowry, there was the equally valuable asset of her prestigious dynastic connections through which the Stuart Cause might also be advanced. In these respects, it's worth bearing in mind that such a marriage might open up the possibility of James Stuart's candidacy for the Polish crown which was elective, and that could be regarded by those states who had an interest in maintaining the Balance of Power, or *status-quo*, as 'an appalling vista'.[50]

---

48 Mclynn, *Bonnie Prince Charlie*, 8–9; Szechi, *The Jacobites*, 108–110.

49 Huss, *Der Wiener Kaiserhof*, 85–90.

50 The phrase, but not its notoriety, is borrowed from the former Master of the Rolls Lord Justice Thomas Denning's controversial judgement quashing a civil action by The Birmingham Six against the West Midlands Police in 1980. It was not until 1989 that their innocence was established in Britain and their convictions were overturned. Denning then admitted that he was wrong, he apologised to the six and their families, and he condemned the West Midlands Police.

Charles VI's Irish Entourage during This Period

In addition to maintaining equilibrium among the powers as well as the personal friendship between the emperor and the elector-king, the very fact that Irish Jacobite commanders and regiments served in both the Bourbon French and Spanish services, and had played significant roles in major victories, many under Berwick's command, over the armies of Charles VI and his allies during the War of the Spanish Succession, would not have inclined the emperor towards benevolence to the Jacobite Cause.[51] In 1717, the emperor agreed to the addition of a separate article to the Treaty of Westminster that required him to expel Jacobites from his domains.[52] How would this affect relations between Charles VI and the significant *Irische Präsenz* in his court and army?

Ever since the late 1620s onwards, Irish émigré nobles and soldiers were present in the Austrian Habsburg establishment. Foremost among them were families such as the Butlers of Roscrea, the Walshs of Carrickmines, the Taaffes of Ballymote, earls of Carlingford, the Hamiltons of Tyrone and Leitrim, and the Brownes of Camus and Knockainy. Within the period of the late 1690s to the 1730s, increasing numbers of Irish officers and soldiers, disillusioned with the Stuarts were attracted by greater opportunities in Spain and elsewhere, a small but significant number of them transferred their allegiance to Austria and the Holy Roman Empire.[53] Irish Catholic bitterness against the Catholic allies of William III, particularly Leopold I or Joseph I, expressed by Irish poets such as Seán Clárach Mac Domhnaill

---

51   Harman Murtagh, 'Irish Soldiers Abroad, 1600–1800', in Tom Bartlett and Keith Jeffrey, eds, *A military history of Ireland*, (Cambridge, 1996), 294–314; Downey 'Beneath the Harp and the Burgundian Cross', 97–101.

52   Alfred Francis Přibram, *Österreichische Staatsverträge*, England, 2 vols, (Wien, 1907 &1913), on Treaty of Westminster I, 333–337 and 338 for the additional anti-Jacobite article in 1717.

53   Murtagh, 'Irish soldiers abroad', 300; Declan M. Downey, 'Die Wildgänze und der Doppeladler. Irische Integration in Österreich von 1630 bis 1918, in Christoph Hatschek, & Michael Kenny, eds, *Die Wildgänze. Irische Soldaten im Dienste der Habsburger*, (Wien, 2003), 43–59.

seems not to have had much effect on the Irish in the Holy Roman Empire.[54] Having been 'worsted in the game'[55] they accepted the new realities. The aforementioned Francis Taaffe provides an example of this attitude when after the Peace of Rijswijk in 1697, at which he represented the interests of Duke Leopold for restoration to Lorraine et Bar, he was received most courteously and amicably by William III at his palace of Het Loo, and was given personal assurance and protection of his Irish titles and properties.[56]

During the War of the Spanish Succession, some of Irish origin in the Spanish establishment wanted to see the Habsburg dynasty continue on the throne and supported Charles, and followed him back to Vienna.[57] Many served under Prince Eugene alongside Elector George in campaigns in the Rhineland and Flanders, as well as in Prince Eugene's liberation of Transylvania, Serbia and Wallachia. Indeed, Eugene and Marlborough were benevolent patrons of the Irish in Austrian and Imperial service. General Count John Andrew Hamilton, Lieutenant Fieldmarshal Count George Oliver Walsh, and Lieutenant Fieldmarshal Count George Browne were three of the most notable among *die Irische Präsenz* in the Court of

54 For example see Sean Clárach Mac Domhnaill's execration of Leopold I and his descendants, Joseph I, Charles VI and Maria Theresa penned after one of Austria's defeats early in the War of the Austrian Succession (1740–1748): ' ... *sin choíche sliocht Leópold faoi cheo na mallacht'* – ' ... *there's Leopold's dynasty forever under a cloud of curses'*, quoted from Vincent Morley, *The Popular Mind in Eighteenth-century Ireland*, (Cork, 2017), 156–161, especially 158–159.

55 Quote taken from the refrain of the traditional Irish song, *Seán Ó Dhuibhir a 'Ghleanna*, written by the priest and author Patrick Augustine Sheehan (1852–1913) on the subject of the Irish Jacobite Army's defeat at the Battle of Aughrim (1691) and subsequent flight to France:

'Ah, but Seán Ó Dhuibhir a Ghleanna,
We were worsted in the game'.

56 Paul de Rapin Thoyras, *Histoire d'Angleterre* (Nancy, 1760), Chapter 'Guillaume III', 519; Downey, 'Die Wildgänze und der Doppeladler', 46–47.

57 Declan M. Downey, 'Whether Habsburgs or Bourbons? Some reflections on the alignments of nobles of Irish origin during the War of the Spanish Succession', in Enrique García Hernán, & Igor Pérez Tostado, eds, *Irlanda y el Atlántico Iberico. Movilidad, participación e intercambio cultural*, (Valencia, 2010), 243–252; Downey 'Beneath the Harp and the Burgundian Cross' 83–105.

Charles VI during the period 1715 to 1720. Hamilton, was general of cavalry, was a particularly close companion and confidant of Prince Eugene and served with him in the War of the Spanish Succession and in the liberation of Belgrade in 1717. Later in 1737, Hamilton became the first of Irish origin to become President of the Imperial War Council in 1736.[58] Walsh had distinguished himself as a commander in the sieges of Temesvár 1716 and Belgrade in 1717, and thereafter in the Battle of Francavillia and the Siege of Messina in 1718.[59] Browne, also gained distinction in the War of the Spanish Succession and in the Turkish War. His influential book on military training and tactics *Der Kriegs Exercitum* was printed for the Austrian Army in January 1717.[60]

There is little evidence to suggest that the Irish who served under Austrian and Imperial colours had much enthusiasm for the Jacobite cause in 1709, 1715 and 1719. They were essentially liegemen who, having lost everything at home found they had a more prosperous future as a 'service nobility' who owed their careers, ennoblements and privileges to the emperor. It would have been most imprudent of them if they were to risk all of that for an exiled claimant who was totally dependent on the emperor's enemies and their tactical games. It remains to be seen if any convincing testimony of personal sympathy among the Irish in the Imperial Court for the Stuart claimant and his intended spouse incarcerated in Innsbrück in 1719 might yet be discovered and presented.

As Austrian and Imperial officers, those of Irish origin could, and some did, return to Ireland as officers of a valued and prestigious ally, a privilege that was not enjoyed by their compatriots who had served Britain's traditional enemies, France and Spain, and were thus specifically targeted for outlawry by the Irish Parliament.[61] Even Catholic clergy who had been

---

58 *Österreichische Staatsarchiv Wien, Hofkriegsrat Akten, Exp. 1718, Mai 213, Hofkriegsrat an Hofkammer und Commisariat, Wien 14 Mai 1718*; Downey, 'Die Wildgänze und der Doppeladler'; Ernst Schmifhofer, *Das Irische, Schottische und Englische Element im Kaiserlichen Heer*, (unpublished D.Phil. dissertation, Universität Wien, 1971), 116–118.

59 O'Donell, *Die Abstammung, Familien und Taten*, 156–157.

60 Christopher Duffy, *The Wild Goose and The Eagle. A Life of Marshal von Browne, 1705–1757*, (London, 1964), 1–20.

61 Éamonn Ó Ciardha, *Ireland and the Jacobite Cause*, 137- 45, 164–166.

educated in Austrian Habsburg Flanders or Bohemia, such as Bishop Francis O'Rourke of Killala, former private chaplain of Prince Eugene of Savoy, could obtain imperial protection on returning to Ireland. In his case, he was received in audience by Queen Anne who gave him safe passage and licence for his ministry. Thus armed, he remained generally unmolested by the authorities in Ireland. His experience was even more remarkable as the Banishment of Popish Bishops Act had been recently passed in the Irish Parliament.[62] Such vignettes require a more nuanced approach towards the study of Irish Catholic émigrés and Jacobitism.

Conclusion

It is evident from the foregoing exposition on the confluence of interests between Hanoverian Britain and Habsburg Austria, as well as the close familial ties between the ruling houses and the personal loyalties between George I and Charles VI, that the emperor would oblige his friend and ally in detaining Princess Maria Clementina Sobieska at Innsbrück, and thereby helping to prevent a strategic marriage for their mutual enemy, the Stuart claimant to the British throne.[63] That dramatic episode occurred in spring 1719, at a crucial time when British naval support for Austrian forces in Sicily was vital. As with all the previous failed attempts by James III & VIII for restoration, in 1709, in 1715 and in 1719, timing and the ebb and flow in the confluence of interests among the European Powers, were against him. It would take a few more years until 1725 before circumstances would change auspiciously enough for the exiled king-in-waiting

---

62 Cathaldus Giblin, 'Irish exiles in Catholic Europe', in Patrick Corish, ed., *A history of Irish Catholicism* IV, pt. 3, (Dublin, 1971), 39.

63 Heinz Duchardt, 'England-Hannover und der europäischen Friede, 1714–48', in Adolf Birke and Kurt Kluken, eds, *England und Hannover* [*England and Hanover*], (Munich and London, 1986), 127–144; Jeremy Black, 'The Revolution and the development of English foreign policy', in Evelyn Cruickshanks, ed., *By force or by default? The revolution of 1688–1689*, (Edinburgh, 1989), 135–158.

to send his representative, Philip Wharton, first Duke of Wharton, to the Imperial Court in Vienna.[64]

Bibliography

Primary Sources

Archives du Ministère des Affaires Étrangères, Paris, Angleterre, 277, ff. 22–6, ff 20–38, 128–33, 150, 226–7, 274–88.
Hannover Hauptstaatsarchiv, iii Calenberg Brief Archiv, II EI, nos. 99, 177, 258.
Österreichische Staatsarchiv Wien, Hofkriegratsprotokoll, 1677, fol.53. HKR an Lothringen.
Österreichische Staatsarchiv Wien, Hofkriegsrat Akten, Exp. 1718, Mai 213, Hofkriegsrat an Hofkammer und Commisariat, Wien 14 Mai 1718.

Secondary Sources

Bergin, Joseph, *The rise of Richelieu* (Yale, 1991, repr. Manchester and New York, 1997).
Black, Jeremy, 'The Revolution and the development of English foreign policy', in Evelyn Cruickshanks, ed., *By force or by default? The revolution of 1688–1689*, (Edinburgh, 1989).
Black, Jeremy, 'When "natural allies" fall out. Anglo-Austrian Relations, 1725–40', in *Mitteilungen des Österreichischen Staatsarchiv*, Vol. 36, (1983).
Brune, Gustav, ed., *Correspondence complete de Madame duchesse d'Orléans née princesse palatine, mère du régent*, 2 vols, (Paris, 1855, 3rd edn 1863).

---

64   Jeremy Black, 'When "natural allies" fall out. Anglo-Austrian Relations, 1725–40', in *Mitteilungen des Österreichischen Staatsarchiv*, Vol. 36, (1983), 120–149.

Chance, J. F., 'The "Swedish Plot" of 1716–7', in *English Historical Review*, Vol. XVIII, (1903).

Corp, Edward, *The Stuarts in Italy, 1719–1766: a royal court in permanent exile*, (Cambridge, 2011).

Daniell, Francis Henry Blackburne, ed., *Historical manuscripts commission, calendar of Stuart Papers*, vols I, II, III, (London, 1902, 1904, 1907).

de Rapin Thoyras, Paul, *Histoire d'Angleterre*, (Nancy, 1760).

Downey, Declan M., 'Beneath the Harp and the Burgundian Cross: Irish Regiments in the Spanish Bourbon Army, 1700–1818', in Hugo O'Donnell, ed., *Presencia irlandesa en la milicia española. The Irish presence in the Spanish Military – 16th to 20th centuries*, (Madrid, 2014).

Downey, Declan M., 'Die Wildgänze und der Doppeladler. Irische Integration in Österreich von 1630 bis 1918', in Christoph Hatschek and Michael Kenny, eds, *Die Wildgänze. Irische Soldaten im Dienste der Habsburger*, (Wien, 2003).

Downey, Declan M., 'Whether Habsburgs or Bourbons? Some reflections on the alignments of nobles of Irish origin during the War of the Spanish Succession', in Enrique García Hernán and Igor Pérez Tostado, eds, *Irlanda y el Atlántico Iberico. Movilidad, participación e intercambio cultural*, (Valencia, 2010).

Duchardt, Heinz, 'England-Hannover und der europäischen Friede, 1714–48', in Adolf Birke and Kurt Kluken, eds, *England und Hannover [England and Hanover]*, (Munich and London, 1986).

Duffy, Christopher, *The Wild Goose and The Eagle. A life of Marshal von Browne, 1705–1757*, (London, 1964).

Fritz, Paul Samuel, *The English Ministers and Jacobitism between the rebellions of 1715 and 1745*, (Toronto, 1975).

Genet-Rouffiac, Nathalie, *Le grand exil: les jacobites en France, 1688–1745*, (Paris, 2007).

Giblin, Cathaldus, 'Irish exiles in Catholic Europe', in Patrick Corish, ed., *A history of Irish Catholicism* IV, pt. 3, (Dublin, 1971).

Goubert, Pierre, *Mazarin* (Paris, 1990).

Griffin, S. J., *The Jacobite diplomats to the court of Emperor Charles VI, 1716–1740: a study in eighteenth century diplomacy*, (unpublished MA dissertation, University of Limerick, 2016).

Guthrie Smith, John and Oswald Mitchell, John, *The old country houses of the old Glasgow gentry*, (Glasgow, 1878), XCIX Wolfe House.

Hatton, Ragnhild, *George I. Elector and King*, (London, 1978).

Henderson, Nicholas, *Prince Eugen of Savoy. A biography*, (London, 1964, repr. 2002).

Hildesheimer, Francois, *Richelieu, une certaine idée de l'état*, (Paris, 1985).

Hill, Brian W., 'Oxford, Boilingbroke, and the peace of Utrecht', in *The Historical Journal*, Vol. 16, No. 2, (June 1973).

Huss, Frank, *Der Wiener Kaiserhof. Eine Kulturgeschichte von Leopold I. bis Leopold II*, (Gernsbach, 2008).

Kamen, Henry, *Philip V of Spain. The king who reigned twice*, (Yale, New Haven and London, 2001).

McGrath, Charles Ivar, 'Securing the protestant interest: the origins and purpose of the penal laws of 1695', in *Irish Historical Studies*, Vol. 30, No. 117, (May, 1996).

McLynn, Frank, *Bonnie Prince Charlie*, (London, 1988).

Morley, Vincent, *The popular mind in eighteenth-century Ireland*, (Cork, 2017).

Murtagh, Harman, 'Irish soldiers abroad, 1600–1800', in Tom Bartlett and Keith Jeffrey, eds, *A military history of Ireland*, (Cambridge, 1996).

Ó Ciardha, Éamonn, *Ireland and the Jacobite cause, 1685–1766*, (Dublin, 2002).

O'Donell, D., *Die Abstammung, Familien und Taten der österreichischen Generäle irisher Herkunft in Siebenjährigen Krieg*, (Universität Wien, Unpublished M.Phil. Thesis, 1998).

Otmar von Aretin, Karl, *Das Reich: Friedensgarantie und europäisches Gleichgewicht 1648–1806*, (Stuttgart, 1986).

Přibram, Alfred Francis, *Österreichische Staatsverträge*, England, 2 vols, (Vienna, 1907 & 1913).

Richard-Maupillier, Frédéric, 'The Irish in the regiments of Duke Leopold of Lorraine, 1698–1729', in *Archivium Hibernicum*, Vol. 67, (2014).

Roberts, Clayton, 'The fall of the Godolphin Ministry', in *Journal of British Studies*, Vol. 22, No. 1 (autumn 1982).

Scharf-Wrede, Thomas, ed., *Katholisch in Hannover; Menschen-Geschichten-Lebenswelten. Quellen und Studien zur Geschichte und Kunst in Bistum Hildesheim*, (Hildesheim, 2019).

Schmifhofer, Ernst, *Das Irische, Schottische und Englische Element im Kaiserlichen Heer*, (unpublished D.Phil. dissertation, Universität Wien, 1971).

Simms, John G., *Jacobite Ireland, 1685–91*, (London, 1969, repr. Dublin, 2000).

Simms, John G., *The Williamite Confiscation in Ireland, 1690–1703*, (London, 1956).

Soons, Alfred H. A., ed., *The 1713 peace of Utrecht and its enduring effects*. Nota et Vetera Iuris Gentium Series, (Leiden and Boston, 2019).

Szechi, Daniel, *1715: the Great Jacobite rebellion*, (Yale, 2006).

Szechi, Daniel, *The Jacobites. Britain and Europe 1688–1788*, (Manchester and New York, 1994).

Tapié, Victor-Lucien, *La politique étrangère de la France et le début de la Guerre de Trente Ans (1616–1621)*, (Paris 1934).

Treasure, Geoffrey, *Mazarin: the crisis of absolutism in France*, (London, 1995).

Williams, Basil, *Stanhope. A study in eighteenth-century war and diplomacy*, (Oxford, 1932, repr. 1968).

Woker, Franz Wilhelm, *Geschichte der Katholischen Kirche und Gemeinde in Hannover und Celle*, (Paderborn, 1889).

EDWARD CORP

6 Clementina Sobieska at the Jacobite Court

The marriage of Clementina Sobieska with the exiled King James III produced two Stuart princes, Charles, Prince of Wales (the future Bonnie
Prince Charlie) and Henry, Duke of York (the future Cardinal York)*.
In all other respects it was a complete failure, and in January 1726, a little
over six years after her wedding, Clementina informed her father that for
the last six years she had been neglected and scorned, and had suffered a
kind of living death.[1]

To understand what went wrong it is necessary to know about the
leading personalities at the exiled court when the marriage was negotiated
in 1718, and in particular to examine the frame of mind of James III himself. Until that has been done one cannot begin to understand the predicament which Clementina faced when she joined the Stuart court at Rome.

---

1   Nacyjanalnyi Gistaeycznyi Archiu Bielarasu w Minsku (National Historical
     Archives of Belarus in Minsk, hereafter NGAB), f.694, o.12, rkps 360, k.182–185,
     Queen Clementina to her father, 19 January 1726: 'Il y a six ans que je souffre
     mort et passion et un mépris si grand, que je ne scaurois vous l'expliquer mais afin
     de ne vous affliger j'ay gardée tout cela dans mon Coeur.' The texts of all the let-
     ters quoted here from this archive are taken from Aneta Markuszewska, 'And
     all this because of "the weakness of your sex": the marital vicissitudes of Maria
     Klementyna Sobieska Stuart, wife of the Old Pretender to the English throne', in
     Almut Bues, ed., *Frictions and failures: cultural encounters in crisis*, (Wiesbaden,
     2017), 163–177. This quotation is at 171.

By 1718 James had suffered a series of terrible disappointments. A planned Franco-Jacobite invasion of Scotland had failed in 1708. His expectation of succeeding his half-sister Anne when she died in 1714 had come to nothing. The Jacobite risings in Scotland and northern England in 1715–1716 had been defeated. He had been forced to leave France, then Lorraine and Avignon, and take refuge in the Papal States, because the French court had withdrawn its support, especially after the death of Louis XIV. And by 1717 he was living in the relatively remote city of Urbino, feeling cut off from direct contact with any princes in Europe who were willing to support him, as well as with the Jacobites in his three kingdoms.[2] In brief, he was emotionally very vulnerable.

He had been brought up in France surrounded by ministers and advisers much older than himself, most of whom were English Catholics who had no recent experience of living in England.[3] In 1716, however, his court was joined at Avignon by several Scottish Protestants who had lived all their lives in both Scotland and England, and some of whom were his own age. Two years later, when he was at Urbino, he turned against his French background and developed a friendship with three of these new Scottish Protestant Jacobite exiles. They were John Hay (a son of the 7th Earl of Kinnoul), Hay's wife Marjory, and Marjory's brother James Murray (a son of the 5th Viscount Stormont). As the weeks and months went by these three Protestants gradually established a virtual domination over the mind of the vulnerable Catholic king, so that by the end of that year the other Jacobite courtiers felt that John and Marjory Hay and James Murray monopolised the king's favour and could do no wrong in his opinion.

Yet James needed for dynastic reasons to get married, and the arrival of a new queen was likely to threaten the recently acquired dominant position of the three favourites, particularly as the queen would be Catholic and they were Protestant. Moreover James was 30 years old, and a strong willed adult lady would probably attempt to reduce their influence. So from their

2   Edward Corp, *A court in exile: the Stuarts in France, 1689–1718*, (Cambridge University Press, 2004).
3   Edward Corp, *The Jacobites at Urbino: an exiled court in transition*, (Palgrave Macmillan, 2009).

point of view an inexperienced 17-year-old girl who spoke no English was an ideal choice, and they naturally encouraged James to accept the recommendation of Charles Wogan that he should select Clementina Sobieska.

From the very beginning it was arranged that Clementina would be confronted by the three favourites. The details of the marriage contract were handled by James Murray in negotiation with her father at Ohlau in Silesia. Then John Hay was sent to accompany Clementina from Silesia to Ferrara, where she would be met by Murray and his sister Marjory. In the event that the king should be unable to travel to Ferrara, Murray was given a warrant to marry Clementina on his behalf by proxy. Even before her marriage took place, therefore, it was intended that the 17-year-old Catholic Clementina should be managed by her future husband's three Protestant favourites.

As we know, the marriage at Ferrara did not take place as planned in October 1718, and Clementina did not meet and marry King James until the beginning of September 1719. What happened during those ten and a half months made Clementina's future prospects even worse. James travelled to Spain at the beginning of 1719 with John Hay, hoping to join a Spanish fleet being sent to invade England. When the fleet was destroyed by a storm James and Hay lived together for three months at Lugo, a small and remote town in Galicia, before returning to Italy to meet Clementina. This bonding experience brought the two men even closer together and made them completely inseparable friends. The result was that Clementina would never be able to come between them. Hay's influence with the king was to be disastrous for her future happiness.

During the king's absence the Jacobite court, which had left Urbino for Rome, was placed under the control of Murray, who then behaved in an arrogant and rude manner towards the Jacobite courtiers, and succeeded in alienating virtually all of them. When they complained, the king regarded their criticisms as threatening to undermine his own authority, so he gave Murray his full support, encouraged by Hay.

One of the chief complaints against Murray was the way that he had been treating Queen Clementina, whom he had married by proxy at Bologna on 9 May, with his sister Marjory Hay as the only Jacobite lady or gentleman in attendance. This gave Murray an inflated sense of his own importance and made him even more arrogant and overbearing. When Clementina arrived in Rome a week later, and was given temporary accommodation by the Pope in the Ursuline convent, Murray refused to allow any of the other Jacobite courtiers to meet her for three whole months, with the obvious exception of his own sister.[4] Eventually, a few weeks after her eighteenth birthday, and with the support of some of the cardinals, she insisted on receiving a visit from some of the senior Jacobites and demanded to see the palace which had been made available for her husband by the Pope. Murray had no option but to give way, but he planned his revenge.

Clementina had arrived in Rome with three valets and three chambermaids from Silesia.[5] Murray responded to his setback by advising King James that all six of them should be sent back to Silesia as soon as possible, so that his sister Marjory Hay and a small team approved by her could be Clementina's only attendants. James and John Hay agreed to this suggestion, although in the end they did allow one of the valets to remain.[6] Clementina privately told Charles Wogan that she 'was very much disgusted

4   Charles Wogan and Eleanor Misset, who were not members of the court, were allowed to visit her. The Duchess of Mar and the Countess of Nithsdale were given very limited access, despite the fact that James had specifically recommended them to Clementina in a letter of 7 February 1719 (Royal Archives at Windsor Castle, Stuart Papers (hereafter RA. SP) 42/14.).

5   The valets included Gottfried Rittel (who already had an Italian wife) and Joseph Weber. The name of the third valet is at present unknown. The chambermaids are described in the parish register of the church of Santi Apostoli as Katherina Kloppelin (who married Joseph Weber on 2 January 1720), Mlle Abraim and Mlle Eleonora (Rome, Archivio Vicariato, Santi Apostoli, vol. 22, 89; and vol. 57, 35).

6   Gottfried Rittel remained and served Clementina until her death, when the queen left many items of her clothing to his daughter. (The inventory is in RA. SP 192/179). James III, who did not wish to admit that the chambermaids had been dismissed, wrote to Prince James Sobieski that 'one of them has married, one of them has no wish to stay, and the third cannot serve by herself because she only speaks German' ('l'une est mariée, une autre ne veut pas rester, et la troisième ne peut pas server seule a cause qu'elle ne scait pas d'autre langue que l'alemande': Markuszewska, p. 167). There is an undated letter in the Gualterio papers from Dame Elisabeth Aberline, wife of Christophe Aberlé (sic) (described as Polish from Vienna), asking the cardinal to help with the education of her two sons, both born at Ohlau (British Library, Add. MSS 20313, f. 288).

with Mr Murray and his sister' and that she 'was not only angry with Mr Murray but despised him'.[7]

Clementina, of course, hoped that King James, whom she met and married formally at Montefiascone at the beginning of September 1719, would support her. But she was rapidly disappointed. Even the wedding ceremony gave an indication of how the marriage would develop, because she was accompanied to Montefiascone only by Murray, Marjory Hay and a small group of Irish servants. Apart from Charles Wogan and Eleanor Misset, these included two men (Colonel John O' Brien and a Dominican friar named John Brown) and one woman (Mary Fitzgerald). There were no English servants to witness the marriage of the King of England, and all the six servants from Silesia were also left behind in Rome. The marriage certificate was signed only by John Hay and James Murray (both Scottish), Wogan, O'Brien and Brown (Irish), and the local Italian vicar general named Sebastiano Antonini.[8] The painting recording the event was actually painted fifteen years later. It shows three ladies in addition to Marjory Hay, and if those ladies were really there they must have been Italian because none of the Jacobite ladies were invited.

Once the marriage had been solemnised, and the 31-year-old James had taken his bride back to Rome at the beginning of November 1719, John Hay used his influence with the king to minimise the queen's position at the Jacobite court. He did this, in collaboration with his wife and Murray, by persuading the king that Clementina, a mere 18-year-old girl, should not be given her own household. As a king living in exile, James had influence but no authority beyond his own royal palace, the Palazzo del Rè, in Rome. He agreed that giving Clementina her own household would erode what little authority he still possessed.[9]

This decision to deny Clementina her own household was the cause of the eventual breakdown of the royal marriage, so it is necessary is to understand why denying Clementina her own household was so important.

7   Corp, *The Jacobites at Urbino*, 200.
8   See Figures 6.1 and 8.2.
9   Edward Corp, *The Stuarts in Italy, 1719–1766: a royal court in permanent exile*, (Cambridge University Press, 2011).

James's own mother, Mary of Modena, had her own household, like previous English queens. This meant that she had selected, appointed, controlled and dismissed her own servants, and that she had her own apartment in the royal palace. It also meant that she had been fully responsible for the care, upbringing and education of her son, that is James himself, until he was 7 years old. Without her own household Clementina had no control over the choice of her servants. Apart from her remaining valet from Silesia, she had chambermaids and washerwomen, all chosen for her by the king, and only one lady of the bedchamber and one bedchamber woman (the two senior ranks in attendance on a Queen of England). The lady was Marjory, wife of John Hay and sister of James Murray. The woman was Captain Misset's wife Eleanor, but *she* was quickly dismissed by Hay and Murray, and not replaced. So Clementina, although recognised in Rome as Queen of Great Britain and Ireland, could only be accompanied inside and outside the palace by Marjory Hay, except when she was with her own husband. And she greatly resented this.

Lacking her own household also meant that she did not even have her own apartment. The royal apartments in the Palazzo del Rè were described as 'the King's apartment', which was where James lived on the first floor, and the joint 'King and Queen's apartment', which was where Clementina lived on the second floor.

Finally, and this was the most important of all, she was not given control over the servants looking after her son Prince Charles, who was born on 31 December 1720. At first, of course, they were all women, selected by the king and answerable to him, though they naturally sympathised with her, and the most senior of them, named Dorothy Sheldon, became Clementina's most active supporter at the court. When Charles was still only 4 years old, however, King James decided to entrust the boy to a small staff of unmarried men.[10] They were at least all Catholic, but this was done in September 1725, two and a half years earlier than was normal.

10   King James has already appointed Francesco Bianchini in 1722, and then the Chevalier Andrew Ramsay in 1724, to be tutors to the prince, but these were in fact no more than nominal appointments as the boy was only 1 year old in 1722 and 3 years old in 1724, much too young to start his formal education. Bianchini was dismissed after a few months (RA. SP 62/5, Creagh to Bianchini, 28 August 1722), and Ramsay had left the court before Charles's fourth birthday (Corp, *The Stuarts in Italy*, 154).

The reason for this was that a few months earlier, in March, Clementina had given birth to Prince Henry and the king wanted to transfer the team of women to look after the new prince. (It was difficult to recruit suitable Jacobite servants so far from the British Isles, and accommodation in the nursery was limited). But this decision was very strongly opposed by the queen and Dorothy Sheldon.[11] Moreover the prince's new servants were placed under the overall direction of a Protestant, because James wanted to emphasise his belief in religious toleration. Clementina was understandably furious, and especially because the Protestant chosen for this position was James Murray (created Earl of Dunbar) whom she detested. To add insult to injury Murray had instructions from the king that Clementina should no longer be allowed to see her son privately, all meetings having to take place in the presence of Murray himself. The reason for this was because James feared that she would influence the boy against Protestants and Protestantism, and it made Clementina, who by then was a mature 24-year-old woman, feel that she had had enough.

In her desperation Clementina was bound to ask who was advising her husband to make these decisions, and the answer of course was Hay (created Earl of Inverness). Hay justified his attitude by sneeringly describing Clementina as 'passion [and] youth ingrafted by a little mean education ..., governed by whim and fancy'.[12] Or, as Clementina complained to her father, Hay and the other two favourites constantly said that she had been given 'a very bad and very disgraceful education'.[13] But Hay had also given Clementina the ultimate insult. He had not only had the effrontery to write a letter to the queen in which he accused her of only disliking his wife Marjory because she believed that Marjory was having an affair with the king, but had himself been 'in a manner making love to [Clementina] by dumb signs and gestures as squeezing of hand, and amorous looks and

---

11　Dorothy Sheldon was one of the three daughters of Ralph Sheldon (equerry to both James II and James III) and Elizabeth (née Dunn). Her sister Catherine was married to Sir Arthur (Jacobite Lord) Dillon; and her sister Frances to Simon Scrope of Danby Hall.

12　Corp, *The Stuarts in Italy*, 144.

13　See note 1: 'ils disait a tous moments que j'avois eüe dans la maison de mon Père une tres mauvais et tres disgraciée education' (Markuszewska, 172).

gestures' indicating that 'he had a desire ... to attempt her honor'.[14] No wonder Clementina wrote to her father that the three favourites had 'neither honour nor religion nor conscience'[15] as well as being 'arrogant and insolent'.[16] By the autumn of 1725 Clementina could take no more and determined to challenge her husband publicly.

To understand the context of what happened next it is necessary to know about Clementina's separation from her family, and particularly her hopes that she and her children might soon be able to leave Rome.

At the end of August 1722, just before she received the insulting letter from John Hay, Clementina received the news that her mother had died. The circumstances of the escape from Innsbruck meant that she had never had the opportunity to say a proper farewell to her mother, whom she had never seen again. Then, in June 1723, she was told that her sister Marie Casimira had died. Her remaining sister Carolina – known as Charlotte – then married the prince de Turenne, heir to the duc de Bouillon, in August 1723 and moved from Ohlau to live at the French court.[17] As all her attempts to persuade her father to visit Rome came to nothing,[18] she hoped that

14   Corp, *The Stuarts in Italy*, 169.

15   NGAB, f.694, 0.12, rkps 358, k.88–89, Clementina to her father, November 1725: 'ils n'ont ny honeur ny religion ny conscience' (Markuszewska, 169).

16   See note 1: 'plus arrogants et plus insolents jusqua dire que je n'avois pas le sens commun et tout ce que je faisoit par un prencipe de devoir, ils disoient que c'etoit la conduitte d'une femme qui avoit l'ame bas, vil et rampant' (Markuszewska, 172).

17   Charlotte's husband died shortly after their marriage, but she then married his younger brother in 1724 and therefore remained the princesse de Turenne. (Her second husband succeeded as duc de Bouillon in 1730). Her portrait was painted in 1724 by Alexis Simon Belle, who signed his name as 'Pictor Regis Britann' (Painter to the British King). The original was sent to Clementina in Rome and is now in the Waters Art Gallery in Baltimore. Belle painted a replica which was sent to the Queen of Spain, Clementina's first cousin, and which is in the royal palace in Madrid.

18   For example, in a letter of 1724 or early 1725 she wrote to her father that 'I am throwing myself at your feet and begging you in the name of God that you should not forsake me, and that you should come, with all possible haste, to visit me. If you want me to live, your presence is necessary to me' ('Je viens me jeter a vos pies pour vous supplier au nom de Dieu de ne me pas abandoner, et de venir me trouver au plutôt, si vous voulés que je vive, car votre presence mest necessaire' : Markusze wska, 168).

circumstances might permit the Jacobite court to leave Rome and return to France where her remaining sister now was. Failing a Stuart restoration to England, her hopes were directed to the possibility of moving to the Château de Saint-Germain-en-Laye, where the exiled court had been situated from 1689 to 1712, and where there were many Jacobites still living. She knew that the Jacobites there were hostile to Hay and Murray, and that they were sympathetic to her. Moreover it would be easier in France to recruit servants from England, and there was much more available accommodation at Saint-Germain in which to house them. And just at this moment it seemed that a move to France was a distinct possibility.

In the summer of 1725 it seemed that the pro-Hanoverian foreign policy conducted by the French government since the death of Louis XIV might at last be about to change, and that the Stuarts might be invited to return to France. The reason for this was that Louis XV was about to marry the Polish Princess Maria Leszczyńska who was one of Clementina's cousins, and it was hoped that she might use her influence to support the claims of the exiled James III. Moreover the French ambassador in Rome, Cardinal de Polignac, expected to be recalled to Versailles to become the new chief minister there, and he let Clementina know that he would do all he could to have James invited back. It was noted by a German living in Rome in August 1725 that Queen Clementina 'has told her close friends that very soon she and her husband will be living elsewhere .... I think these are hopes raised by Cardinal de Polignac of their going soon to France, something that [she] passionately longs for'. Shortly afterwards the German noted, 'I have learned that the marriage of the King of France to the Polish Queen who is a relation of Princess Sobiesky [sic] has considerably raised the hopes of [King James] and his supporters.'[19]

At the beginning of October, however, very bad news was received in Rome. A new alliance had been signed between the governments of Great Britain and France, confirming that French foreign policy would remain pro-Hanoverian and anti-Jacobite. The new Queen of France had not acquired any significant influence, Cardinal de Polignac was not to return to Versailles, so the Stuarts would not be invited to leave Rome and return to

19   Corp, *The Stuarts in Italy*, 72–73.

Saint-Germain. Clementina's hopes were dashed, and she began to think of a way to escape from her husband and the Jacobite court.

During October it was reported that there was 'a great dispute ... between Lord Dunbar governor of the elder boy and the women who had brought the boy up until now and who are trying to play a part in his education'.[20] The leader of the women in this dispute was Clementina's friend Dorothy Sheldon, and in November she was dismissed from her position and ordered to return to France for being openly rude to the king. For Clementina this was the last straw, and she had a furious argument about it with her husband in front of their servants in the Palazzo del Rè. She also made three demands: that John and Marjory Hay should be sent away from the court; that James Murray should be replaced as Prince Charles's governor by someone else, who should be a Catholic; and that she should be given her own household, so that she could select and appoint her own servants, including of course her second son's governor. When James refused, on the grounds that doing so would undermine his authority within the Jacobite court, Clementina made her decision to leave him and take refuge in the convent of Santa Cecilia in Trastevere.[21]

The Jacobites sided almost entirely with Clementina, if only because the Hays and Murray were so unpopular. But opinion in Rome was divided. On the one hand the pope and many cardinals supported Clementina because the three favourites were Protestant, and they believed that Prince Charles should have a Catholic governor. On the other hand many believed that it was proper for James to be master of his own family and that it was Clementina's duty as a wife to obey her husband. When an eventual compromise was reached, enabling Clementina to leave her convent and return to the court, it mainly reflected this second point of view. John and Marjory Hay, realising how unpopular they were, agreed voluntarily to leave the court. The queen was given her own household, but her servants

20   Ibid., 163–164.
21   She was joined in the convent by Dorothy Sheldon (who had refused to leave Rome), Gottfried Rittels's daughter, and her two loyal Scottish chambermaids. Dorothy Sheldon had been so rude to James III that he eventually arranged for her to be sent away to live in the convent of San Pietro Martire in Bologna, where she remained until her death in 1763 (RA. SP 140/133 and 415/145).

were all selected and appointed by her husband. And Murray not only remained the governor of Prince Charles, but was also made governor of Clementina's second son Prince Henry when he too was only 4 years old.

The marriage of James and Clementina never recovered, and she became a recluse within the Palazzo del Rè. She devoted herself almost entirely to her Catholic religion, became (as far as we can judge) anorexic, and died when she was still only 33 years old.

Living in Rome, the centre of the Catholic church, her life was ruined by the influence of her husband's three Protestant favourites. James was only living in exile because he refused to convert to Protestantism, but by falling under the influence of Protestants he fatally destroyed both his chances of a successful marriage with his Catholic wife and the happiness of his two young sons. Clementina was beautiful and popular, and full of enthusiasm when she travelled from Silesia, and escaped from Innsbruck to get married in Italy. Yet within only a few months all her enthusiasm had been crushed by her husband's favourites, who treated her with disdain as though she were of no consequence – as she put it 'as if I had been the lowest of creatures'.[22]

In marked contrast to the evidence contained in her letters, the portraits of Queen Clementina painted between 1719 and 1725 tell a different story. Far from showing the lowest of creatures, or 'la derniere des creatures' to use her own words, these portraits show an exceptionally beautiful woman looking poised and thoroughly regal. If she was treated as badly as she maintained, and there is no reason to doubt that, then these portraits bear witness to the tragedy of her life at the Jacobite court, and show us the impressive appearance of the queen to whom the king's three Scottish favourites showed such a lack of respect.

There are so many portraits of Queen Clementina which date from 1719 to 1725 that great care is necessary to separate the original ones commissioned by the king from the many replicas, copies and variant copies, particularly in miniature, and the numerous engravings and the paintings copied from those engravings. Careful study has shown that Queen

22   See note 1: 'j'ay été traitée avec autant de hauteur comme si j'avais été la derniere des creatures' (Markuszewska, 172).

Clementina sat for seven original portraits during the first six years of her marriage during which, as she told her father, she felt that she was neglected and scorned and suffered a kind of living death: in her own words again, 'je souffre mort et passion et un mépris si grand'. These seven portraits were painted by Francesco Trevisani and Antonio David in 1719, by Girolamo Pesci in 1721, by David again in 1722 and 1723, and by Martin van Meytens (the Younger) in 1725. There might perhaps have been other portraits, but if so they have not survived.[23]

The first portrait was painted by Francesco Trevisani in the spring of 1719, shortly after Clementina arrived in Rome and while King James and John Hay were in Spain. It shows her standing beside a table on which there is the closed crown of a queen. Her left hand holds a fan, while her right hand is firmly placed on top of the crown. Her pink dress, her bodice and her belt are generously decorated with jewels, and she also wears over her shoulders an ermine lined blue cloak. Her clothes and her hair are styled according to the prevailing fashion of the time. Clementina looks radiantly beautiful and is portrayed as the Queen of England, but it is clear that she is only 17 years old and she looks vulnerable. The portrait was painted to be given to her future husband (Figure 6.2).

23   Edward Corp, *The King over the water: portraits of the Stuarts in exile after 1689*, (National Galleries of Scotland, 2001); and *The Stuarts in Italy*, chapters 5 and 14.

Figure 6.1:　Agostino Masucci, *The Solemnisation of the Marriage of King James III and Queen Clementina at Montefiascone on 1 September 1719*, 1735

Agostino Masucci, *The Solemnisation of the Marriage of King James III and Queen Clementina at Montefiascone on 1 September 1719*, 1735, 243.5 x 342 cm, oil on canvas (National Galleries Scotland). There is a small copy of this picture in the sacristy of the cathedral at Montefiascone. The painting was also engraved twice by Antonio Friz, and one of his engravings (much inferior to the other) is reproduced in Sharp, *The Engraved Record*, p. 214. It is not possible to establish with certainty the identities of the people shown in the picture, apart from Marjory Hay, the king and the queen, Father John Brown (in profile immediately above the queen) and Sebastiano Bonaventura (the presiding bishop). The gentlemen kneeling behind the king are presumably (left to right) John Hay, Charles Wogan and Colonel John O'Brien (all of whom signed the marriage certificate), and the gentleman pointing on the right is presumably James Murray (who had married Clementina by proxy and who also signed the certificate). Murray and O'Brien were the only ones still at the Stuart court when the picture was painted in 1735.

Figure 6.2: Francesco Trevisani, *Queen Clementina*, 1719, 25.8 x 19.4 cm, oil on
copper (private collection). The three original versions of the portrait are lost, but this
copy was painted at the time for Lord Richard Howard. There are two bust copies by
Antonio David in private collections, and two full sized copies made from the original
in the Palazzo del Rè by William Mosman in 1733 and by Francesco Bertosi in 1735,
one of which is in the Scottish National Portrait Gallery (98 x 73 cm). The portrait was
not engraved.

Later that same year the queen was painted by Antonio David. This
portrait was intended to be sent away to Paris to be engraved and then
circulated in multiple copies to the Jacobites at home and abroad so that
they could see their new queen. Clementina stands beside another table
on which a crown has been placed, but this time her hand has not been
placed on it. Her dress is different, and it bears fewer jewels, but she again
wears an ermine lined blue cloak. She still looks young, but the painter

has made her look a little older so that the engravings would not quickly become dated (Figure 6.3). She looks as beautiful as she did in the portrait by Trevisani, and there seems no reason to believe that she is anything but happily married.[24]

Figure 6.3: Queen Clementina 1719

Pierre Drevet after Antonio David, Queen Clementina, 1719, engraving 43.2 x 31 cm.

24 There are replica copies of the portrait at Lambeth Palace in London and Chiddingstone Castle in Kent, and the former is reproduced in Corp, *King over the water*, 60. There are several copies in miniature as well as a bust copy. The portrait was engraved in reverse by Pierre Drevet, and his engraving is reproduced in Richard Sharp, *The engraved record of the Jacobite Movement*, (Aldershot, 1996), 105.

By the spring of 1720, when she was 18 years old, Clementina was pregnant, so no new portrait was commissioned during that year. In the spring
of 1721, however, by which time she had given birth to Prince Charles, her
husband commissioned Girolamo Pesci to paint two new portraits of her,
one to be displayed in the Palazzo del Rè in Rome, and the other to be sent
to her first cousin the Queen Dowager of Spain at Bayonne. In the first she
is seated on a throne with the little prince sitting on a small chair beside her,
and in the other she is by herself again standing beside a table (Figures 6.4
and 6.5). Both portraits show her with a crown (in the first it is placed on
top of the back of the throne, and in the second it is placed on the table),
but both include her familiar blue ermine lined cloak.[25] What strikes one,
however, about these two portraits is how she has matured and is beginning
to look more like a young woman than the 19-year-old girl that she still
was when they were painted. As Queen of England she outranked all the
other ladies in Rome and was greatly admired by the pope, the cardinals
and the princely families of Rome. One could not possibly guess from
looking at these portraits that she was not considered worthy to have her
own household within the Palazzo del Rè. And it should be stressed that
John Hay's dismissive remark that she was 'passion (and) youth ingrafted
by a little mean education ..., governed by whim and fancy' was written in
the very same month that these two portraits were painted.

25   These portraits are respectively at Stanford Hall in Leicestershire and the Prado
      Museum in Madrid, and both of them are reproduced in Corp, *The Stuarts in
      Italy*, 101–102, and *King over the water*, p. 61. There is a miniature copy of the one
      at Stanford Hall by Pesci himself, and a bust copy made by John Smibert in 1721.
      Neither of the original portraits was engraved.

Figure 6.4: Queen Clementina

Girolamo Pesci, Queen Clementina and Prince Charles, 1721, 167.6 x 116.8 cm, (Stanford Hall).

In the autumn of 1722 King James commissioned David to paint another portrait showing Clementina as Queen of England. It shows her wearing an ermine lined dress, with a double string of pearls attached to her right shoulder and elegantly falling towards her left hip. On the front of her dress there is a delicate floral design, while beside her shoulder there is a crown. This time the ermine lined cloak is a golden yellow rather than blue. Clementina, now 21 years old and the mother of a little boy, is unquestionably a young woman rather than a girl (Figure 6.6). The portrait was neither copied nor engraved, so we may assume that it was displayed in the king's own apartment in the Palazzo del Rè. This was the time when Clementina was continuing to be treated with disdain by John Hay and his wife Marjory.

Figure 6.5: Queen Clementina

Girolamo Pesci, Queen Clementina, 1721, 102 x 80 cm, (Prado, Madrid).

In the following year, 1723, King James decided to commission several sets of paired portraits of himself and his wife to be sent away as gifts to some of his more important Jacobite supporters. He therefore instructed David to paint a similar portrait of Clementina, but this time showing her looking to her left to match one of himself looking to his right. These portraits are both busts and omit the crown, to make it safer for Jacobites to display them in England and Scotland, and the one of Clementina shows her in a different dress without the floral design on the front, and without any pearls. Her face, however, is the same as in the portrait painted the previous year.[26]

Figure 6.6: Antonio David, *Queen Clementina*, 1722, 81.3 x 64.8 cm, oil on canvas (Baltimore, Walters Art Gallery). There are no known copies of this portrait, which was not engraved.

---

26 There are two known versions of this portrait, both of them in private collections. One of them is reproduced in Corp, *King over the water*, 63. A version of this

By the summer of 1724 Clementina was again pregnant, so no new portrait was painted that year. In the summer of 1725, however, shortly after giving birth to Prince Henry in March, King James commissioned a new portrait by Martin van Meytens. This was done immediately before the care of Prince Charles was entrusted to a small staff of unmarried men, before the Protestant James Murray was appointed to be the little boy's governor, and before Clementina was told that she could no longer see her 4-year-old son except when Murray was also present. The portrait therefore shows Clementina as she was immediately before she had the public row with her husband in front of the assembled courtiers in the Palazzo del Rè, and which resulted in her leaving the court and taking refuge in the convent of Santa Cecilia in Trastevere.

The original portrait by Meytens, which was displayed in the king's own apartment, does not seem to have survived, but the composition is extremely well known because it was copied many times by a great many painters, including Antonio David in 1730 (cover image), Ludovico Stern in 1740, Louis-Gabriel Blanchet in 1740 and 1741, and Domenico Duprà in 1742. It was also reproduced in mosaic in 1741 as part of Clementina's monument in the basilica of St Peter's at the Vatican. Clementina wears an ermine lined red cloak with a strip of blue material falling from her right shoulder to her left hip and a large jewelled brooch pinned to the front of her bodice. The crown is not included in this portrait because, like the previous one by David, it was intended to be copied many times and given away to be safely displayed in Great Britain as well as on the continent.

By 1725 Clementina was 23 years old, and the portrait by Meytens shows her as a mature woman, the mother of two young boys. She remains beautiful and there is absolutely nothing in this portrait to indicate how profoundly unhappy she was and how close to leaving her husband and taking refuge in the convent. There is, however, a clue that all was not well. The king's treasurer commented that the portrait showed Clementina 'fuller in the face' than she really was and that it did not therefore 'resemble' her as well as it 'should have done'.[27] In her distress and unhappiness Clementina had begun to eat less: she was perhaps already becoming anorexic. Despite the evidence of this portrait, therefore, she was slowly beginning to become thinner and to lose her radiant beauty.

---

portrait was engraved by John Faber and Andrew Miller in 1737, both reproduced in Sharp, *The engraved record*, 107.

27   Corp, *The Stuarts in Italy*, 112.

The next portrait was painted two years later, in March 1727, by which time Clementina had been living an austere life in the convent of Santa Cecilia for one and a half years. And it is so different to all the previous ones! It shows her modestly dressed and in mourning, holding a breviary beside her crown. She has lost weight and her face, so full and beautiful in Meytens's portrait of 1725, is now pinched and thin (Figure 6.7). Clementina ordered several copies to be made of the portrait (of which at least six are known to have survived) to indicate how badly she had been treated, and that she would not return to the court until the three Scottish favourites had been dismissed and she had been given her own household.

Figure 6.7: Antonio David, *Queen Clementina*, 1727, 43 x 32 cm, oil on canvas (private collection). This version of the portrait was painted for Sir David Nairne. It shows the book held by the queen to be above the table, whereas the other known copies, which all measure approximately 73 x 61 cm, show the book with its spine resting on the table. The portrait was not engraved.

Unfortunately for Clementina she did not get what she wanted. A compromise settlement was reached which enabled her to return to the court, but she had very limited control over her newly established household, and Murray remained the governor not just of Prince Charles but of Prince Henry as well. As a result Clementina shut herself off in her apartment and took no part in the life of the court, so consequently she was never again painted wearing the clothes of a courtier. This meant that the portrait of 1725 by Meytens had to be reproduced over and over again whenever the king wanted to give someone a set of four portraits showing the Stuart royal family. Clementina did, however sit, or rather kneel, for some more portraits before her early death in January 1735 when still only 33 years old. There is a large full-length portrait of 1730 by Pierre-Charles Trémolières showing her at prayer before a crucifix and an open breviary;[28] another of 1734 by Domenico Muratori in which she is shown half-length pointing at the crucifix but without a breviary;[29] and a posthumous one of 1735 by Agostino Masucci which shows her full length holding her breviary and kneeling before an altar on which is placed a monstrance which transfixes her gaze (Figure 6.8).[30] These three pictures all include the closed crown of the Queen of England, and in all of them Clementina is wearing her ermine lined blue cloak over a simple dress. She is no longer beautiful, her hair is combed back into a simple bun, and in the last one she looks surprisingly old for her years.

28   This portrait measures 194 x 147 cm and is in a private collection in France.
29   The portrait is lost, but was engraved by Girolamo Rossi in 1734 and is reproduced in Sharp, *The engraved record*, 109.
30   The portrait is lost, but was engraved by Miguel de Sorello in 1737 and is reproduced in Sharp, *The engraved record*, 24.

Figure 6.8: Queen Clementina

Miguel de Sorello after Agostino Masucci, Queen Clementina, 1735, engraving of 1737, 27.8 x 19.5 cm.

Memories of how young and optimistic Clementina had been when she escaped from Innsbruck in 1719 were nevertheless kept alive by the portraits by Trevisani, David, Pesci and Meytens which were still displayed in the

Palazzo del Rè. In 1735 Masucci was commissioned to paint a second post-humous of the queen, this time showing her at Montefiascone having her marriage to King James solemnised by Bishop Bonaventura before a select crowd of clergy and courtiers. In both portraits Masucci has Clementina kneeling beside the same cushion and beside an identical crown and sceptre, but this time he has copied the image of the young queen from the 1719 portrait by Trevisani. While Clementina demurely looks down as James places her wedding ring on a finger of her left hand, Marjory Hay stands threateningly behind her in a dark coloured dress. And standing beside the altar, while everyone else is looking at James and Clementina, James Murray arrogantly looks away and merely points towards the ill-fated couple whose marriage he would do so much to undermine (see Figure 6.1). The painter has provided a fitting commentary on what Clementina Sobieska would soon experience at the Jacobite court.

Bibliography

* Surviving correspondence between Clementina's Sobieski uncles Alexander and Constantine in the National Historical Archives at Minsk has shown that Clementina was born in 1701, not in 1702 as previously believed. One of their letters of 1701 even expresses disappointment that their sister-in-law (Hedwig Elisabeth, wife of Prince James Sobieski) had given birth to a girl, Clementina, rather to than a boy. (I am grateful to Professor Aleksandra Skrzypietz of the University of Silesia at Katowice for this information).

Primary Sources

Archivio Vicariato, Rome, Santi Apostoli, vols 22 & 57.
British Library, London, Gualtiero Papers, Add. MSS 20313, f. 288.
Royal Archives, Windsor Castle, Stuart Papers 42/14; 192/179; 62/5; 140/133; 415/145.

Secondary Sources

Corp, Edward, *A court in exile: the Stuarts in France, 1689–1718*, (Cambridge University Press, 2004).

Corp, Edward, *The Jacobites at Urbino: an exiled court in transition*, (Palgrave Macmillan, 2009).

Corp, Edward *The King over the water: portraits of the Stuarts in exile after 1689*, (National Galleries of Scotland, 2001).

Corp, Edward, *The Stuarts in Italy, 1719–1766: a royal court in permanent exile*, (Cambridge University Press, 2011).

Markuszewska, Aneta, 'And all this because of "the weakness of your sex": the marital vicissitudes of Maria Klementyna Sobieska Stuart, wife of the Old Pretender to the English throne', in Almut Bues, ed., *Frictions and failures: cultural encounters in crisis*, (Wiesbaden, 2017).

Sharp, Richard, *The engraved record of the Jacobite Movement*, (Aldershot, 1996).

ANETA MARKUSZEWSKA

7 Political Allusions in Music Dedicated to James Stuart and Maria Clementina in 1719

The wedding of Maria Clementina Sobieska and James Francis Edward Stuart (the Old Pretender) was among the most notable and celebrated social and political events in Europe in 1719. It gave new impetus to the Stuart cause, as King George I faced the frustratingly plausible prospect of new Stuart descendants with a claim to the British throne arriving on the political scene to challenge his rule. Emperor Charles VI was likewise displeased, and both rulers made robust, though ultimately unsuccessful, efforts to frustrate the union. On her way to Italy Maria Clementina was stopped and detained in Innsbruck, from which she was spirited away by a group of courtiers loyal to the Stuarts led by Charles Wogan. The daring escape was much talked about, from aristocratic salons all the way down to lowly inns. The union between Sobieska and Stuart was favoured by Pope Clement XI, Maria Clementina's godfather, who was hoping that their marriage would not only lead to a restoration of the Stuart dynasty, but also, more importantly, bring England back into the fold of the Roman Catholic Church. With so much hanging on the success of that project, the pope and others were willing to invest large sums of money and make considerable efforts and sacrifices on its behalf.

Maria Clementina and James Stuart were married in two separate ceremonies. The first, held in Bologna soon after Sobieska's arrival in the city, was held by proxy because James was not in Italy on account of his involvement in a renewed restoration attempt involving a Spanish invasion of England by sea, and an uprising in Scotland. Following the military defeat of his supporters, James returned to Italy and the second ceremony (a solemnisation) was held again in person at the beginning of September in the private chapel of Bishop Bonaventura's palazzo opposite the cathedral at Montefiascone, an important location for English Catholics at the time (Figure 6.1).[1] In this article I will be mainly focusing on Maria Sobieska, a young person who found herself rapidly catapulted into public life with all its political entanglements in Rome and Europe. I will look at the interesting aspects of how the image of Maria Stuart as a Queen of England was being projected in Rome. I will be relying on contemporary journals, diaries, letters and above all on propagandist musical compositions dedicated to the newly wedded couple in 1719 to identify the political allusions they contain.

Sobieska arrived in Rome in May 1719. The June issue of *Mercurio Storicoe Politico* included the following announcement:

> On the 13th day of the foregoing month, that Princess arrived in Rome in the carriages of the Pretender, who styles himself King of England, and whom, as they say, she had married by proxy in Bologna. She was greeted outside the Gate (Porta del Popolo) by Cardinals Gualtieri and Acquaviva, and by other persons of high rank, who moved aside after exchanging the first greetings; after that, the Cardinals took her to the Ursuline monastery, where an apartment had been prepared for her, and where she was given a great deal of *rinfreschi* on behalf of the Pope and Cardinals Gualtieri and Acquaviva.[2]

During the early days, which Maria Clementina spent at the Ursuline convent, she received visits from Church officials and ladies of Rome as well as taking excursions to the city with a large retinue. Efforts were made to treat her like royalty on each of those occasions. On her visit to the Capitol 'she was greeted by the sound of trumpets and drums, and with all the honours usually afforded to crowned heads'.[3] The same happened

---

1   Edward Corp, *The Jacobites at Urbino: an exiled court in transition*, (Basingstoke, 2009), 138.
2   *Mercurio Storico e Politico*, June 1719.
3   *Mercurio Storico e Politico*, July 1719.

on her visit to the English College with Cardinal Gualtieri[4] where she was 'waited upon like a queen'. The choice of those musical instruments was not accidental. Trumpets, mentioned first in the account, were customarily used as 'manifestations of majesty, heroism, and kingly might',[5] an excellent musical setting to honour a person perceived as the rightful Queen of England. On her visit to the Capitol, the director of the French Academy, Charles Poerson, added: 'The Princess carried herself admirably on that occasion, as on all others. She is highly praised on account of her lively, beautiful spirit, said to be founded on discernment that would be admirable even in a person older than her years.'[6] This short remark suggest that Maria Clementina's early days in Rome were a public relations success.

Birthday Compositions

In June 1719 Maria Clementina was waiting for James to arrive in Rome, and she celebrated his birthday with 'a solemn mass and the singing of a *Te Deum* in the church of the Ursuline monastery where she had taken residence'.[7] James Stuart's birthday, 10 June, was one of the most important dates for his followers, who used it to stage demonstrations of loyalty to the Stuart cause.[8] Sobieska quickly realised the date's importance in

---

4   Cardinal Gulatiero Bassetti was Cardinal-Protector of England during this period. He is alternately referred to as Cardinal Gualtiero or Cardinal Gualtieri in various sources.

5   Steven E. Plank, *Trumpet and horn*, in Stewart Carter, and Jeffery Kite-Powell, eds, *A performer's guide to seventeenth-century music*, 2nd edn, (Bloomington and Indianapolis, 2012), 133.

6   Anatole de Montaiglon, ed., *Correspondance des directeurs de l'Académie de France à Rome avec le sur intendants des bâtiments* [*Correspondence of the directors of the Academy of France at Rome with the superintendent of the buildings*], vol. v, (Paris, 1889), 244.

7   *Mercurio Storico e Politico*, June 1719.

8   Paul Kléber Monod, *Jacobitism and the English people, 1688–1788*, (Cambridge, 1989), 210.

Jacobite propaganda and celebrated it with full commitment. In July, co-
inciding with Maria Clementina's own birthday, the French journal *Le
Mercure* reported a solemn mass celebrated at the Ursuline church with
choral accompaniment. A cantata was dedicated to Sobieska on that occasion, with a libretto by Francesco Bianchini and music (sadly lost) by
Giovanni Giorgi, *maestro di cappella* at the Archbasilica of St John of
Lateran. The title page of the printed libretto reads:

> CANTATA /FOR THE BIRTHDAY/of Her Sacred Royal Highness of Britain /
> CLEMENTINA /QUEEN OF ENGLAND etc. /*Which alludes to the union of two
> stars, known as blessed ones, which took place on 17 July 1719. The Cantata was held at
> the Academy and printed in Rome in 1687 by Her Late Royal Highness,/ Christina of
> Sweden/* to welcome a diplomatic mission sent to the Holy See / upon the ascension
> to the Throne of England of His Majesty / KING JAMES THE SECOND, /of
> glorious memory. / [It] shows the sentiments of that celebrated Oration / and the
> words spoken in verse and composed on that occasion / by Royal Academicians /
> DEDICATED TO HER MAJESTY OF BRITAIN /By Montsignore Francesco
> Bianchini, Servant of Honour to His Holiness.[9]

We should note that Maria Clementina is styled 'Queen of England'
on the title page, an appellation which will reappear in other librettos and
operas dedicated to her over the years. This is one indication of how successive popes and municipal authorities of Rome viewed the Stuarts. The
use of the royal title in greetings and dedications makes it clear that the
couple is recognised in Rome as rightful rulers. The long title also refers
to an *academia* held at the residence of Queen Christina of Sweden in the

---

9   CANTATA/ PER IL GIORNO NATALIZIO/ Della Sacra Reale Maestà
     Britannica/ DI/ CLEMENTINA/ REGINA D'INGHILTERRA &c./ In
     cui si allude alla unione delle due stelle, dette benefice,/ che accade in quell dì
     17. Luglio 1719. ed all'/Accademia tenuta, e stampata in Roma/ l'anno 1687.
     dalla Maestà della fu/ Regina CHRISTINA DI SVEZIA. /In occasione della
     solenne Ambasciata, spedita alla S. Sede/ nell'assunzione al Trono d'Inghilterra
     della Maestà/ DEL RE' GIACOMO SECONDO./ Di gloriosa memoria,/ Con
     riferirsi i sentimenti della célèbre Orazione,/ e le parole de'Versi allora composti/
     dalli Accademici Reali/ DEDICATA A SUA MAESTA' BRITANNICA./
     Da Monsignore Francesco Bianchini Cameriere d'Onore /di Nostro Signore.
     Biblioteca Casanatense, I-Rc Vol. Misc. 932.

presence of the English ambassador sent to Rome on the occasion of the ascension of James II, Maria Clementina's father-in-law.[10] The text is a literary pasticcio: the print explains that verses printed in italics were taken from a cantata written in honour of the ambassador, and those in inverted commas were originally part of a speech made during the *accademia*.

Bianchini wrote the cantata in a complicated, somewhat turgid style, but the text makes use of interesting tropes and formal conceits. First, it makes deft use of the figure of Astrea, goddess of justice. A winged star-maiden bathed in light and depicted with a halo around her head and a flaming torch in her hand, Astrea was a daughter of Zeus and Themis, who descended from the heavens during the Golden Age to teach humanity about the virtues of justice and order. Dismayed by human iniquity during the Iron Age she left the earth and returned to the heavens, where she took her place in the constellation of Virgo. In the libretto Astrea is so delighted with young Maria Clementina that she returns to earth and ties the marital knot between her and James Stuart *due benefichestelle* and restores rightful political order on earth. As the goddess of justice, Astrea notes that James III and his wife are the rightful rulers of Britain and decides to return the usurped kingdom to the couple.

Second, the librettist used the birthday of Maria Clementina not only to allude to her own high birth, but predominantly to highlight the royal past of the family she was marrying into. In this context, he uses a reference to the diplomatic mission sent to the pope by James II, her late father-in-law, upon his accession to the English throne in 1685.[11] At a personal level,

10   RELAZIONE/ DELL'ACCADEMIA/Solennizata nel Real Palazzo/DELLA REGINA DI SVEZIA/Il secondo, il settimo e il nono/giorno di Febraro 1687/ Per festeggiare Affunzione al Trono/DI/GIACOMO SECONDO/RE D'INGHILTERRA/In occasione della folenne Amhasciata mandata/dalla M.S. alla Santità di Nostro Signore/ INNOCENZO XL, (Rome, 1687). See also, *Accademia per Musica, per Lord Castlemain* [*Academy for Music, for Lord Castlemain*] (1687), in Giovanni Morelli, ed., *L'invenzione del gusto. Corelli e Vivaldi. Mutazioni culturali, a Roma e Venezia, nel periodo post-barocco* [*The invention of taste. Corelli and Vivaldi. Cultural mutations, in Rome and Venice, in the post-Baroque period*], (Milan, 1982), 49–66.

11   ACCADEMIA/ PER MUSICA / Fatta nel Real Palazzo/ Della Maestà Della Regina /CHRISTINA / Per festeggiare l'Assonzione al Trono / DI /GIACOMO II / RE D'INGHILTERRA,/ in occasione della Solenne Ambasciata mandata /

the pope may not have been impressed with the ambassador in question, who found himself entangled in a series of scandals, but Queen Christina of Sweden held a splendid academy in his honour, recorded in numerous sources including chronicles, a published account of the celebrations, a print of the speech addressed to the ambassador; and a printed libretto which states that a cantata by Bernardo Pasquini was performed during the *accademia*, featuring an orchestra made up of 150 instrumentalists led by Corelli. Thus, the reference also connected Sobieska's arrival in Rome to Christina of Sweden's memorable stay in the city.

In quoting a passage from a speech once made by Cardinal Albani, now Pope Clement XI and a supporter of the newlyweds, Bianchini was alluding to another important aspect of the Stuart project, namely religion. In his speech at that famous *accademia*, Albani referenced the biblical story of Abraham and Sarah, a couple he described as refugees who had to leave their lands to follow God's calling; the story now became a transparent allusion to James Stuart, who had spent nearly all of his life away from England and considered himself a king in exile.[12] But the biblical story went even further in that it highlighted the fact that James and Maria Clementina were true Christian believers. The story of Abraham and Sarah was also a benediction in that it alluded to a story of good fortune and fertility as a wish to perpetuate the Stuart dynastic project.

Gennaro Angelini, a nineteenth-century Italian scholar who wrote an article about Maria Clementina, writes that following the performance

---

da Sua Maestà Britanica alla Santità/ di Nostro Signore / INNOCENZO XI, / Roma 1687, I-MOe 70.i.15.1; ORAZIONE / IN LODE / DI / GIACOMO II / RE DELLA GRAN BRETAGNA &c. / DIFENSOR DELLA FEDE./ Detta nella Accademia degl'Infecondi di Roma / DA DONATO ANTONIO LEONARDI, /ALL'ILLUSTRISS. ET ECCELLETNISS. SIG. / CONTE DI CASTELMAINE / AMBASCIADORE STRAORDINARIO / DI SUA MAESTÀ BRITTANICA / ALLA SANTITÀ DI NOSTRO SIGNORE / PP. INNOCENZO XI, (Rome, 1687).

12   Discorso/ Detto nella Reale Accademia/ Della Maesta di/ CRISTINA/ Regina di Svezia/ in lode di/ GIACOMO II/ Re della Gran Bretagna/ Da Monsignore/ Gio. Francesco Albani/ Accademico Reale/ Innanzi al. Fest oso, e solenne applauso Musicale/ fatto nella medesima Accademia/ sù l'istesso argomento, (Rome, 1687).

of the cantata the guests were invited to a sumptuous meal at which Maria Clementina sat under a canopy. After the meal, a composition by Giorgi was performed. If Angelini's account is accurate (he provides no bibliographic sources), Rome extended a truly royal welcome to the young Maria Clementina, no doubt to James Stuart's satisfaction.[13]

Journey to Montefiascone

The entry for 9 September in the *Diario di Chracas* states that one week earlier, after visiting the pope at 9 a.m., Sobieska set out to Montefiascone to meet with her husband there. Not much information survives about the wedding celebrations. The *Storia di Montefiascone* offers the following facts:

> The following evening after the wedding a holy musical oratorio was presented in the Cathedral, performed by excellent musicians; and the following [evening] the seminarians and college students performed a theatre play (*teatra le rappresentanza*) in their *liceo* for the royal couple. Aside from that, they [the Stuarts] turned down any other solemn manifestations that the city authorities had in mind.[14]

The October issue of *Mercurio Storico e Politico* included a report that Maria Clementina's wedding gift for her husband was a 'bejewelled walking stick, and he gave her a precious jewel of great value, which he had been given in Madrid.'[15] The French *Le Mercure* reported that the gift was 'a diamond-studded dagger which her grandfather, [King] Jan III Sobieski, found after his relief of the Siege of Vienna in the chest of the Grand Vizier'.[16] With evident satisfaction, the English *Weekly Journal or Saturday's*

13   Gennaro Angelini, *I Sobiesky e gli Stuards in Roma* [*The Sobieski and the Stuarts in Rome*], in *La Rassegna Italiana*, Vol. iii, (1883), 163.

14   Luigi Pieri Buti, *Storia di Montefiascone scritta e corredata di molti inedita documenti* [*History of Montefiascone written and corrected from many unedited documents*], (Montefiascone, 1870), 244.

15   *Mercurio Storico e Politico*, December 1719.

16   *Le Mercure*, December 1719. Also seized from among the Grand Vizier's abandoned possessions was a priceless carved turquoise snuff box, mounted in gold,

Post, a publication sympathetic to the Stuart cause, published the following note on 19 September 1719: '[...] the Pretender is not only arrived at Rome, but that he has consummated his Marriage with the Princess Sobieski at the Palace of Cardinal Albani with great deal of ceremony, the Cardinal having treated them with all possible Magnificence.'[17]

The musical composition performed to celebrate the wedding was an oratorio entitled *S. Maria Maddalena de' Pazzi*. The title page of the libretto states:

S. MARIA MADDALENA/ DE' PAZZI/ Oratorio a quattro Voci / Fatto Cantare da Monsignor / SEBASTIANO POMPILIO BONAVENTURA / VESCOVO DI MONTEFIASCONE, E CORNETO/ ALLA PRESENZA / DELLE REALI MAESTÀ / DI GIACOMO TERZO / RE DELLA GRAN BRETAGNA, / E / MARIA CLEMENTINA/ SOBIESCHI / DI LUI REGIA CONSORTE/ IN MONTEFIASCONE, MDCCXIX.[18]

In hindsight, the choice of St Maria Maddalena de' Pazzi as the centre-piece of their wedding celebrations seems woefully prophetic. Following a period of separation from her husband, which began late in 1725, and after spending almost two years in the monastery of Santa Cecilia in Trastevere, Maria Clementina was a changed woman. She spent her final years in prayer, mortification of the flesh, fasting, or with her sons. She died in a state of emaciation at the age of 33, and very nearly joined the ranks of the 'holy anorexics', as documents preserved in the Archivio di Stato in Rome indicate that an effort was launched in the 1740s to arrange for Maria Clementina's beatification.[19] In the end, the beatification process never came to anything, but the pope commemorated her with a tomb and a

---

which remained in the Sobieski family until Prince James Louis presented it as a gift to Charles Wogan on 1 January 1719 at Ohlau. See Cathy Winch, *The rescue of Princess Clementina (Stuart)*, (Belfast, 2008), 51.

17   *Weekly Journal or Saturday's Post*, 19 September 1719.

18   Biblioteca Casanatense, I-Rc, Vol. Misc., 1335 (16).

19   *Processus ordinaria auctoritate costructus super asserto miraculo a deo per intercessionem del famula Maria Clementina Sobieski Regina Magna Britannia* [*Process of ordinary authority over the alleged miracle from God through his servant Maria Clementina Sobieska Queen of Great Britain*], Archivio di Stato di Roma, Tribunale del Cardinal Vicario, busta (vol.) 338.

statue in St Peter's Basilica. In this way Maria Clementina became one of the major female figures in the history of Rome and the Catholic Church. It is worth querying therefore who Maria Maddalena de' Pazzi was.

Figure 7.1: Santa Maria Maddalena De' Pazzi – Oratorio a quattro Voci: Title Page of Oratorio dedicated to King James III and Queen Clementina, 1719

This is the title page of an oratorio dedicated to King James III and Queen Clementina in 1719. It was performed in Montefiascone specifically to commemorate their union.

Introducing St Maria Maddalena de' Pazzi

Maria Maddalena de' Pazzi was born in Florence on 2 April 1566 as
Caterina de' Pazzi.[20] She came from an old and powerful Pazzi family
whose ancestry stretched far back into the Middle Ages. Caterina was
the only daughter of Camillo di Geri de' Pazzi and his wife Maria Buon
del Monti, and she had three brothers. She was viewed as good marriage material, but the girl showed different inclinations from an early
age. Remarkably pious and sensitive to stories about the life of Christ,
Caterina enjoyed spending time in solitude and prayer.

At the age of 14, she was sent to a monastery to get an education. She
quickly came to surpass the sisters in religious fervour and developed early
symptoms of an eating disorder we would now call anorexia. At the age of
16 she completed her trial period and, to her parents' great dismay, entered
the monastery of Santa Maria degli Angeli.

At first her conduct caused problems to her monastic community and
her spiritual superior. However, her idiosyncrasies were quickly recognised
as signs of great spirituality, piety and attachment to God. Caterina, who
chose Mary Magdalen to be her monastic name, refused food for extended
periods of time, sought to mortify her flesh in various ways, and experienced
exhausting episodes of religious ecstasy, which her fellow sisters recorded.
Maria Maddalena died in 1607. The Church of Rome used her influence
by making her the patron saint of the Counter-Reformation (she was be-
atified in 1626 and canonised in 1669).

Eric Dingwell, the late British anthropologist and author of the 1962
study *Very Peculiar People: Portrait Studies in the Queer, the Abnormal and
the Uncanny* described her behaviour as 'a classic example of the ascetic
female flagellant and masochistic exhibitionist with now and then, as might
be expected, a slight sadistic streak'.[21] Rudolph M. Bell, who invented the

---

20   This biographic information on Maria Maddalena de' Pazzi is based on Clare
     Copeland's book, *Maria Maddalena de' Pazzi, The Making of a Counter-
     Reformation Saint*, (Oxford, 2016).

21   Eric Dingwell, *Very peculiar people: portrait studies in the queer, the abnormal and
     the uncanny*, (New York, 1962), 127.

term 'holy anorexia', was more charitable, noting that 'Illness now emerges as the main theme of holy anorexics' lives – how they are visited by God with strange, painful maladies; how they suffer and thereby grow spiritually; how death ultimately allows them to fully embrace their bridegroom in heaven. Illness becomes the alternative to heresy, sorcery, or insanity as the male clerical explanation of holy anorexic behaviour.'[22] This choice of heroine for the oratorio would not have been surprising for a holiday or a religious event. But why was it accepted in a secular context as a fitting subject for celebrating a marriage ceremony with strong political overtones? I will get back to this question later.

Pamphili's Libretto

The libretto of *S. Maria Maddalena de' Pazzi* was not a new work composed specifically for the wedding of James Stuart and Maria Clementina Sobieska. Instead, the verses were taken from an earlier libretto by Cardinal Benedetto Pamphili, who had formed an interest in the life of that saint at an earlier date. On 9 June 1687 his libretto, set to music by Giovanni Lorenzo Lulier, was performed at the Cardinal's residence at Via del Corso in Rome to celebrate an anniversary of the investiture of Francesco Maria de' Medici, a fellow cardinal with whom Pamphili was on friendly terms.[23] From that moment on, Pamphili's libretto was set to music by various composers – not only by Lulier, but also by Carlo Francesco Cesarini and Alessandro Scarlatti, and it was presented in several Italian cities including Modena, Ferrara, Florence, Bologna and also in Vienna. In 1705, Pamphili offered to reuse the story of Maria Maddalena to celebrate another member of the Medici family, namely Grand Duke Cosimo III of Tuscany, who was in Rome at the time.

---

22   Rudolph M. Bell, *Holy anorexia*, (Chicago and London, 1987), 172.
23   Duccio Pieri, ' *"Santa Maria Maddalena de'Pazzi". Origine e diffusione di un oratorio musicale* [*"Saint Maria Maddalena de' Pazzi". Origin and dissemination of an orotario*], in Piero Pacini, ed., *Maria Maddalena de' Pazzi*, (Florence, 2007), 156.

Cosimo III apparently did not care much for music and public honours and turned down Pamphili's dedication. Instead, Pamphili chose to dedicate his libretto to Sister Maria Grazia, a Carmelite nun and a relative of the reigning Pope Clement XI. On that occasion the cardinal made some changes to the earlier 1687 text. Among other things, he removed an allegorical introduction that featured Rome, Time and Religion (Roma, il Tempo, la Religione), altered several lines and generally abridged both parts of the oratorio, primarily by removing the second stanzas from arias. The revised version of the oratorio was performed under the same title with music by Carlo Francesco Cesarini at the Collegio Clementino in Rome, of which Pamphili was a patron.[24] That version of the libretto then formed the basis for the composition performed to celebrate the wedding of James Stuart and the granddaughter of King Jan III.[25]

Regrettably we do not know who set Pamphili's text to music on that occasion. It has been conjectured that it might have been Alessandro Scarlatti,[26] but that conjecture is not supported by any sources. We only know at this point that the oratorio was performed by respected musicians (*scelti professori*) who were invited to perform by the bishop of Montefiascone, Sebastiano Pompilio Bonaventura. The castrato Pasqulino Tiepoli, one of James's favourite singers, was one of them.[27]

In writing the libretto the Cardinal drew on a biography of St Maria Maddalena by one Father Cepari (*Vita della sera ficavergine S. Maria Maddalena de' Pazzi ...*, Rome 1659). The oratorio begins at the point when the young woman decides to join a monastery and faces opposition from her dismayed parents. Four characters appear in the libretto: Maria Maddalena, her mother and father, and Amor Divino (Divine Love). The

24   Ibid.; Claudio Sartori, *Ilibretti italiani a stampa dalle origini al 1800* [*Italian books in print from their origins to the 1800s*], (Cuneo, 1990).

25   As far as I know, a single copy of the libretto has survived in the Biblioteca Casanatense in Rome, I-Rc Vol. Misc. 1335 (16).

26   Santa Maria Maddalena de' Pazzi, Montefiascone, Stamperia del Seminario, 1719 [Montefiascone, Seminary Printworks, 1719], available at <http://corago.unibo.it/libretto/0001010471> accessed on 30 July 2020.

27   Edward Corp, *The Stuarts in Italy 1719–1766. A royal court in permanent exile*, (Cambridge, 2011), 79.

storyline in the libretto is very static, with practically no action to speak of. It runs as follows:

> Maria Maddalena talks to her parents, who are dismayed by her decision to join a monastery. The way they see it, they are losing a much-loved daughter. This is shown in the following recitative and aria by Maria Maddalena:
>
> Rec.: Oh frustrated desired! My hopes were in vain.
> Aria: I hoped that my eyes
> Would be closed by you alone;
> That hope is no more:
> I could yet hope for that;
> But our hearts are guilty,
> Yours of not enough, mine of too much love.

Hearing her mother's words, Maddalena calls for God's help. Her parents' feelings cause her anguish, undermining her strength and determination. Amor Divino appears to Maddalena, and rebukes her for harbouring too many worldly affects in her heart. The woman takes strength from his admonishment, but she is still disquieted by her parents' lamentations. Ultimately Amor Divino overcomes her hesitation, and assures her that she will find peace if she turns her gaze to God. This part concludes with Maria Maddalena's last farewell to her parents; she realizes that she must forsake their love and embrace suffering to follow God's calling.

PARTE SECONDA:

From a distance, Maria Maddalena hears the voices of her beloved parents. She is anguished and hesitant: isn't the love of her parents a good thing? Amor Divino tells her to keep her faith strong. Maria Maddalena reflects on steadfast faith, and Amor Divino reminds her that faith without good deeds is dead. Maria Maddalena remembers that it was her heart's desire to suffer: 'Vogliopene di morte, e non morire' ('I want the pain of death, but not to die'), she exclaims. Great strength fills her, and Maria Maddalena is now ready to act and to embrace suffering. Ultimately, Amor Divino helps her parents accept their daughter's decision, and they ask her forgiveness. Maria Maddalena is happy to see their change of heart. She is surrounded by heavenly light. Amor Divino crowns her with a crown of roses and lilies, a jewel of Paradise that is a gift from her Divine Spouse. The family is reconciled. Maria Maddalena declares her perpetual devotion to Divine Love, and embraces suffering, in which she finds solace.

I wish to suffer because my cries
and sufferings bring comfort.

Hence if my sighs
become my joy;
My God, what shall I do?
Let pains be pains:
Or maybe find a new suffering,
Which to this ardent heart
Shall be new and singular.

This brings me back to the question I raised in the beginning: why should Maria Maddalena de' Pazzi, of all people, have been viewed as a suitable figure for celebrations on a political occasion like a royal wedding? That problem must have also troubled the author of the dedication, who justifies that decision at length.

The opening words of the dedication mention Montefiascone:

> the town should consider itself blessed since heaven elected it for the two splendid turtledoves [Maria Clementina and James Stuart] to alight there for their nuptials. There is nothing accidental about that union, but rather it is decreed by heaven, desired and commanded by Eternal Wisdom. The man and wife are so close emotionally and so deserving of each other, the text strongly suggests, that their souls must have known each other already in the immortal realm, before they descended to enter their earthly bodies. A union this perfect can never be separated in this world, so this joyous occasion needs to be celebrated with divine songs.[28]

The dedication then praises the libretto by Pamphili for the wit and pleasant style in its portrayal of the saint's experience. The text goes on to say:

> it might seem inappropriate to put together religious vows and a royal wedding: that the obscurity of a monastery, where a lonesome soul lives, ill-matches the splendours of your majesties, on which the eyes of almost the whole universe are resting. But it is not so. An epithalamion about a saintly virgin summoned by Divine Love to her marriage in Paradise is a fitting way to celebrate the marriage vows taken by souls filled with God and assisted by Grace [...].[29]

28   *S. Maria Maddalena de' Pazzi*, 3–4.
29   Ibid., 6.

The organisers of the wedding celebrations concluded that the figure of Maria Maddalena de' Pazzi, a female saint treated by the Church as something of a Counter-Reformation trophy figure, was a fitting subject for celebrating the wedding of James Stuart, a Catholic whose cause was supported by the Roman Curia, and Maria Clementina, also a Catholic and a granddaughter of the famous Vanquisher of the Turks. The message here is that their faith is as steadfast as that of St Maria Maddalena, who regarded God as her Beloved and Divine Spouse. The subject matter of the oratorio was therefore an unequivocal declaration of Stuart allegiance to Roman Catholicism.

The dedication also includes wishes of good political fortune, including numerous offspring and, most importantly, successful reclamation of the throne, 'Great and beautiful souls, nothing can darken your carefree peace: reason guided by human law hastens to restore the crown owed to you on earth.'

The newlyweds stayed at Montefiascone until the end of October, enjoying entertainments organised by local authorities in the town and around it. They would later maintain correspondence with the town's authorities. Clementina also made some gifts to be displayed as ornaments in the local cathedral. The liturgical robes she sent to the local clergy have been preserved to this day.

Christmas Trionfi

In 1676, the Apostolic Palace in Rome started a tradition that would continue until 1740, consisting in holding performances of a pastoral cantata around Christmas.[30] On that solemn occasion, the pope would invite to his palace cardinals, members of the papal court, foreign rulers and

---

30 Carolyn Gianturco, '"Cantate Spirituali e Morali" with a Description of the Papal Sacred Cantata Tradition for Christmas 1676–1740', in *Music & Letters*, Vol. 73, No. 1, (1992), 8.

diplomats who happened to be present in the Eternal City, and members of the aristocratic families of Rome. On those nights, works by celebrated composers such as Alessandro Scarlatti, Francesco Gasparini, Antonio Caldara, Flavio Anicio Olibrio, Giuseppe Ottavio Pitoni and many others were played, and sumptuous dinners were served.

The Christmas cantatas performed at the Apostolic Palace were didactic and moralising in character. Carolyn Gianturco writes that they mostly used the joyful theme of the adoration of baby Jesus by the shepherds. Here was a story about the origins of Christianity that could also serve as a reminder of its most important rules. 1719 was no exception. A three-part cantata was performed at the Apostolic Palace with a libretto by Andrea Diotallevi and music, sadly lost, by Giovanni Giorgi, who also composed the birthday cantata dedicated to Sobieska.[31] There were three characters in that piece: Angel (Angelo) and two shepherds named Erasto and Daliso. With the assistance of the angel, who reveals religious truths to the shepherds, Erasto and Daliso find the place where Jesus is born. The piece has a joyful mood filled with happiness, simplicity and refinement, and it shows nature that resonates with the feelings of the providentially chosen group of people. Sadly, the names of the singers who performed the cantata have been lost as well.

The author of the *Diario di Chracas* devoted considerable attention to the celebrations taking place at the Apostolic Palace in 1719. The Stuarts received a remarkable gift in the form of so-called *trionfi*, or marzipan sculptures of various scenes, characters and objects that were used as table decorations during papal feasts. Because this tradition is interesting, and the *trionfi* sent the next day to the Stuarts' palace were reportedly quite magnificent, I include here, in its entirety, a description of the *trionfi* published in the *Diario*, in Carolyn Gianturco's English translation:

---

31 CANTATA / DA RECITARSI / Nel Palazzo Apostolico / LA NOTTE / DEL / SS.MO NATALE / NELL'ANNO MDCCXIX. / COMPOSTA / DA ANDREA DIOTALLEVI / MUSICA / DEL SIGNOR GIOVANNI GIORGI / Maestro di Cappella della Basilica Lateranense / IN ROMA, MDCCXIX. / Nella Stamparia della Reverenda Camera Apostolica. Biblioteca Alessandrina, I-R, Misc. Ant. XIII.b.2.10.

The first of [trionfi] represented a royal throne with two royal seats, on the first of which sat Christ crowned as King, with robes and royal cloak and with scepter in his left hand; on the second [seat] was the Church dressed as Queen, who, in the act of kneeling, received the ring from his spouse, Christ. At Christ's foot two angels knelt, each with a tray, in one of which were three imperial crowns, and in the other the scepter; & next to the [female] spouse was a standing angel, who held the tablets of Moses in his left hand, & in the right the book of Gospels: on the top of the said triumph one saw the Eternal Father with the Holy Spirit in a glory of cherubs, with the motto HODIE COELEST SPONSO JUNCTA EST ECCLESIA written in large letters.[32]

This spectacular gift and the solemn tones of the cantata symbolically brought to an end the first eventful and emotional year in the marriage of Maria Clementina Sobieska and James Stuart. The surviving information suggests that the authorities in Rome did everything in their power to ensure that the newly arrived Maria Clementina was treated officially as the Queen of Great Britain (Regina di Gran Bretagna).

Maria Clementina attracted considerable interest from the very beginning. Her daring escape from Innsbruck, where she acted with great courage and bravery, invited comparisons with her warrior grandfather, King Jan III of Poland, and it was felt that she had earned her royal status with her courageous comportment on that occasion. It was consistently emphasised that Maria Clementina and James Stuart were Catholics, a fact that may not have won James many new adherents but nonetheless served as an important element in Rome's propaganda efforts. Despite her young age, Maria Clementina was able to win the admiration of many influential people in those early months of her stay in Italy. She was praised for her beauty, grace, education and conversational skills in several languages, as well as her precocious maturity. Maria Clementina seems to have made a successful transition to her new status as a public person. Although her family was known in Europe and her family's wealth was the stuff of legends (one reason why James Stuart took an interest in her), she had in fact been raised at a small German court. We know little about her education and early life. Her father, Jakub Sobieski, made fruitless efforts to revive the family's fortunes and win back the power, influence and wealth it once

32   Gianturco, 'Cantate Spirituali e Morali', in *Music & Letters*, 8.

possessed. He, too, was tempted by the vision that his daughter might become a queen. In the event, Maria Clementina did not disappoint, and was able to effortlessly align herself with the Stuart cause and the policies of the Roman Curia in the early years of her stay in Rome.

Fortunately, too, Sobieska did not forget the music that was dedicated to her in 1719. In the years which followed she showed herself to be a very musical person, deeply fascinated and interested in Roman musical culture. Together with James, Maria Clementina became a patron of one of the most elegant and important opera theatres in the Eternal City, Teatro d'Alibert (Teatro delle Dame). For the Stuarts, great composers as Francesco Gasparini, Nicola Porpora or Leonardo Vinci composed operas to libretti by Antonio Salvi, Apostolo Zeno and to new and fresh verses by Pietro Metastasio. These were works of great power, enormous influence and eternal beauty which still make the Stuart name resonate today.

Bibliography

Primary Sources

Archivio di Stato di Roma, Tribunale del Cardinal Vicario, busta [volume] 338.
Biblioteca Alessandrina, I-R, Misc. Ant. XIII.b.2.10
Biblioteca Casanatense, I-Rc, Vol. Misc., 1335 (16).
Le Mercure, December, 1719.
Mercurio Storico e Politico, June & July 1719.
Weekly Journal or Saturday's Post, 19 September 1719.

Secondary Sources

Accademia per Musica, per Lord Castlemain (*1687*), in Giovanni Morelli, ed., *L'invenzione del gusto. Corelli e Vivaldi. Mutazioni culturali, a Roma e Venezia, nel periodo post-barocco* [*The invention of taste. Corelli and Vivaldi. Cultural mutations, in Rome and Venice, in the post-Baroque period*], (Milan, 1982).

Angelini, Gennaro, *I Sobiesky e gli Stuards in Roma* [*The Sobieski and the Stuarts in Rome*], *La Rassegna Italiana*, Vol. iii, (1883).

Bell, Rudolph M., *Holy Anorexia*, (Chicago and London, 1987).

Buti, Luigi Pieri, *Storia di Montefiascone scritta e corredata di molti e inedita documenti* [*History of Montefiascone written and corrected from many unedited documents*], (Montefiascone, 1870).

Copeland, Clare, *Maria Maddalena de' Pazzi, the making of a counter-reformation saint*, (Oxford, 2016).

Corp, Edward, *The Stuarts in Italy 1719–1766. A royal court in permanent exile*, (Cambridge, 2011).

de Montaiglon, Anatole, ed., *Correspondance des directeurs de l'Académie de France à Rome avec le surintendants des bâtiments* [*Correspondence of the directors of the Academy of France at Rome with the superintendent of the buildings*], (Paris 1889).

Dingwell, Eric, *Very peculiar people: portrait studies in the queer, the abnormal and the uncanny*, (New York, 1962).

Duccio, Pieri, '"Santa Maria Maddalena de'Pazzi". Origine e diffusione di un oratorio musicale [*"Saint Maria Maddalena de' Pazzi". Origin and dissemination of an orotario*]', in Piero Pacini, ed., *Maria Maddalena de' Pazzi*, (Florence, 2007).

Gianturco, Carolyn, ' "Cantate Spirituali e Morali" with a description of the Papal Sacred Cantata Tradition for Christmas 1676–1740', in *Music & Letters*, Vol. 73, No. 1, (1992).

Kléber Monod, Paul, *Jacobitism and the English people, 1688–1788*, (Cambridge, 1989).

Sartori, Claudio, *I libretti italiani a stampa dalle origini al 1800* [*Italian books in print from their origins to the 1800s*], (Cuneo, 1990).

Plank, Steven E., 'Trumpet and horn', in Carter, Stewart, and Kite-Powell, Jeffery, eds, *A performer's guide to seventeenth-century music*, 2nd edn, (Bloomington and Indianapolis, 2012).

Winch, Cathy, *The rescue of Princess Clementina (Stuart)*, (Belfast, 2008).

ESTELLE GITTINS

8 Princess Clementina's Marriage Certificate and Other Jacobite Relics in the Library of Trinity College Dublin

There has been a Library at Trinity College Dublin since the college was founded in 1592, and collecting has been continuous since that time. The Book of Kells, whilst the most famous item, is just one of thousands of collections documenting people, places and institutions often with no connection to Ireland. This short paper will comment on two documents of interest housed by Trinity College Dublin which would be of special interest to scholars of Jacobite history in Ireland. Of particular interest to readers of this collection of essays is the first piece, which was the result of Princess Clementina's liberation and escape.

The Marriage Certificate

The Library of Trinity College Dublin holds two fascinating and little-known Jacobite 'relics', a pair of manuscripts bought by a nineteenth-century Irish tourist in Rome. One is a volume of the private devotions of the last reigning Stuart monarch James II (1633–1701), while the other is the marriage certificate of his son, 'the Old Pretender' James III (1688–1766) and the Polish Princess Maria Clementina Sobieska (1701–1735). Both are intimate family documents that share a remarkable, unbroken provenance reaching back to James III's son, Henry,

Cardinal Duke of York (1725–1807): Henry was the brother of Bonnie
Prince Charlie (1720–1788), and the last of the Stuart line.

Figure 8.1: Minerua, *Pope Clement XI (Giovanni Francesco Albani), 1649–1721*

Minerua, *Pope Clement XI (Giovanni Francesco Albani), 1649–1721*, unknown date, 26.90 x 19.80 cm, line
engraving on paper, (National Galleries Scotland). This engraving depicts Pope Clement XI berobed and
capped with an authoritative look. The papal tiara and crossed keys of the pontifical office are over the
trimonzio and star of the Albani family of Urbino underneath his image, flanked on either side by cherubim.

The marriage certificate (TCD MS 7574) of James III and Maria Clementina is an elaborate object. It is bound in gilded leather with the papal coat of arms of Pope Clement XI on the front displaying the papal tiara and crossed keys of the pontifical office over the trimonzio and star of the Albani family of Urbino (see Figure 8.1). The back cover of the object depicts the royal coat of arms of the House of Stuart. Its crowned escutcheon contains the lion rampant of Scotland, three lions passant guardant of England, three fleurs-de-lys of France and harp of Ireland. Both coats of arms on front and back are ornately and intricately bordered with trailing flowers and cherubim bearing trumpets. Figure 8.2 shows the frontispiece of the marriage certificate depicting the Stuart and Sobieski coats of arms combined on a single crowned gold-bordered escutcheon symbolising the union of both families. The words around the edge of the escutcheon are 'Honi soit qui mal y pense' which translate as 'Shame on he who thinks evil of it'. It is the medieval motto of the chivalric Order of the Garter, which was the most senior order of knighthood in the British honorary system. The escutcheon support is a haloed figure in a golden robe. She is accompanied by a cherub bearing a chalice, its gaze fixed on the cross atop the crown. The village of Montefiascone is most likely depicted below, flooding the lower part of the frontispiece with light as if to signify that the union would bring light to the clouded fortunes of the Stuart kingdoms, who were then under what many considered the illegitimate rule of George I. At the very bottom of the frontispiece there is a depiction of turned soil with sewn crops sprouting from a fertile earth. This echoes an ancient notion that only if the land is governed by legitimate royalty would the natural world function correctly and sustain the kingdoms. The page border is elegantly decorated with colourful trailing flowers and leaves. The certificate itself is mostly printed in Latin but key pages are scribed in ink. Figure 8.3 depicts a page from the certificate where the names of those present are recorded by the hand of a scribe. The certificate is endorsed and initialed by Queen Maria Clementina of Great Britain at the top of the page. The witnesses at the wedding ceremony are inscribed below; two Scotsmen, John Hay and James Murray; and two Irishmen, Charles Wogan and John O'Brien. Beneath the witnesses appears Sebastiano Antonini, local Italian vicar general and protonotary Apostolic. At the bottom of the page Father

Figure 8.2: The Marriage Certificate of James Stuart III and Queen Maria
Clementina Sobieska

TCD MS 7574, *The Marriage Certificate of James Stuart III and Queen Maria Clementina*, courtesy of the
Board of Trinity College, the University of Dublin. The document is bound in gilded leather with the coat
of arms of Pope Clement XI on the front, and that of the House of Stuart on the back, ornately and intricately bordered with flowers and cherubim. In this figure the Stuart and Sobieski coats of arms are shown
combined under a single crown, born aloft by a haloed figure in a golden robe. She is accompanied by a putto
bearing a chalice, its gaze fixed on the cross atop the crown. The village of Montefiascone is most likely that
depicted below, with a fertile earth producing bountifully in the immediate foreground. The page is bordered with beautiful floral decoration. The document was mostly printed in Latin.

Figure 8.3: The Marriage Certificate of James Stuart III and Queen Maria
Clementina Sobieska

TCD MS 7574, *The Marriage Certificate of James Stuart III and Queen Maria Clementina*, courtesy of the
Board of Trinity College, the University of Dublin. The document is bound in gilded leather with the coat
of arms of Pope Clement XI on the front, and that of the House of Stuart on the back, ornately and intricately bordered with flowers and cherubim. This figure depicts a page from the document where the names
of those present are recorded by the hand of a scribe. Queen Maria Clementina of Great Britain is scribed at
the top and the witnesses at the wedding ceremony scribed below: John Hay, James Murray, Charles Wogan
and John O'Brien. Sebastiano Antonini, Protonary Apostolic and Father John Brown are scribed at the
bottom of the page.

John Brown, confessor to King James, listed as present and as a witness. That no English subject of the King of England was represented on the certificate is significant. The painting by Agostino Masucci of the marriage depicts all of the above (see Figure 6.1). That the union took place at all is nothing short of remarkable given the events that led up to it which played out like a Hollywood blockbuster: the details have been covered elsewhere in this volume.[1]

The Dethroned King

The second of the two manuscripts (TCD MS 3529), the book of private devotions of James II, is a small volume of letters, prayers and memoirs written in James' own hand and mostly dated 1698–1700, eight years on from his defeat at the Battle of the Boyne. It is written in English and French. James was then nearing the end of his life and his daughter Mary, and her husband William of Orange, occupied his former throne. The volume provides a window into the former king's psychological state and pious obsessions whilst living in exile in Saint-Germain-en-Laye. While many of the devotions are written in English, some passages are in French. In one part, James proffers advice to an unidentified recipient on how best to spend leisure time: in a nutshell, through prayer, meditation and the reading of good books; also acceptable are affairs of business, moderate hunting, shooting and tennis (but only for the purposes of exercise and the pursuit of desirable company). He especially advises against balls (not the tennis variety), and also censures operas and plays but concedes that 'if obliged at any tyme to go to any of them, to govern ones [eyes] with discretion, and to let ones thoughts be of the vanity of them'.[2]

---

1   See chapter 3. For recent publications about the rescue see Winch, C., *The rescue of Clementina Stuart*, (Belfast, 2008); see also Canavan, T., 'Making a hole in the moon: the rescue of Princess Clementina', *History Ireland*, Vol. 1, No. 4, (winter 1993); Clare Lois Carroll, *Exiles in a global city: the Irish and Early Modern Rome*, 1609–1783, (Leiden, 2017), 232–256.
2   *Trinity College Dublin*, MS 3529.

The Irish Collector

Both of these manuscripts passed into the hands of the last surviving Stuart claimant to the British throne, Henry, Cardinal Duke of York. On his death, in Rome in 1807, most of the Stuart state papers in his possession were purchased by the British government. Some of the more personal items, including his grandfather's book of devotions and his parents' marriage certificate, remained with members of the cardinal's Roman circle. In the decades that followed however, these were sold off in piecemeal fashion to foreign tourists.

The purchaser of the Trinity manuscripts was Blayney Townley Balfour (1799–1882), the fourth of that name of Townley Hall in Drogheda: his father Blayney Townley Balfour III (1769–1856) an Irish MP, built Townley Hall. The family was well used to foreign travel (one brother died in Honduras, another in India) and Blayney himself was Lt-Governor of the Bahamas between 1833 and 1835. After his return to Ireland, he became, like his father before him, High Sherriff of County Louth in 1841. He married Elizabeth Catherine Reynell of Westmeath in January 1843. In the intervening year, he travelled to Rome, where he purchased a series of important items connected to the exiled Stuarts, including a number of personal effects, three portraits and the two manuscripts under discussion. Balfour wrote short accounts of his purchases, including the following which was transcribed by his son, Blayney Reynell Townley Balfour (1845–1928), for a 1925 publication of the volume of devotions of James II,

> 1842. The things in this drawer were purchased by me this spring from the Marquis Malatesta in an old house at the foot of the Capitol stairs. He inherited them from an uncle, an intimate friend of the Cardinal York's, who left them to him. They are relics of the Stuart family. The book of devotions had never been brought out of the family till it left Cardinal York's house. Lady Bray bought a full-length picture at the same time. BTB June.

'Lady Bray' was Sarah Otway-Cave (1768–1862), 3rd Baroness Braye, who also purchased a large number of Stuart portraits from the Malatesta family, the bulk of which remain at the family seat of Stanford Hall,

Leicestershire. Townley Balfour's son also goes on to state that 'among the other relics purchased by my father were three portraits – of Prince James the Chevalier, Prince Charles Edward and Cardinal York. There was also the marriage certificate of Prince James and Maria Clementina of Poland.' One of these portraits, a shoulder-length pastel likeness of a man in armour, by Maurice-Quentin de la Tour, with the same provenance as the Trinity manuscripts, appeared at auction in 1994. Purchased by the Scottish National Portrait Gallery (NGS PG2954) as depicting Charles Edward Stuart it seems to have been the source of numerous presumed likenesses of the Young Pretender. It was, however, the subject of a high-profile re-evaluation by Bendor Grosvenor in 2008 that persuasively re-identified the sitter as Charles' brother, Henry. It is known that, between 1746 and 1747, both he and his brother sat for de la Tour. This took place before Henry's cardinalship and would explain why he was depicted in military attire.

As regards the other items purchased in Rome in 1842, we cannot know the full extent of what might have been kept in the drawer mentioned in Townley Balfour's description, but in other accounts he makes reference to a Stuart-owned pencil case and riding whip. Furthermore, a seal,[3] an amber flask and a scent bottle belonging to the Cardinal are all listed as having been purchased by Townley Balfour from the Malatesta family in Bernard W. Kelly's *Life of Cardinal York* published in 1899.

What impelled Townley Balfour in his purchase of such Jacobite 'relics'? Was this simply a case of a tourist snapping up collectables with a celebrity appeal, or does the episode reveal a deeper sympathy for the Jacobite cause? Despite the Protestant faith of the Townley Balfour family of Drogheda, they were an offshoot of the Towneleys of Towneley Hall near Burnley in Lancashire, one of the major Catholic families of the north of England and renowned as staunch supporters of the Stuarts. Two generations of the Lancashire Towneleys took part in the Jacobite Risings of 1715 and 1745; Francis Towneley (1709–1746) was executed for his part in

---

3   The seal referred to is the bloodstone seal of James II depicting the royal Stuart arms and dated to 1685, which was later acquired by Hever Castle in Kent in 2000 (HCW 1406/0600).

the 1745 Rebellion, and the family reputedly kept his decapitated head in a secret recess in the Towneley Hall chapel. There are other suggestions of Townley Balfour's Catholic sympathies, not least in the existence of a number of seventeenth-century family portraits by the artist Garrett Morphy (c.1655–c.1716) who was known to favour commissions from eminent Catholic patrons. There is also the inclusion of a number of books and pamphlets on the Catholic faith and the penal laws in the Townley Hall library at Drogheda, which is now housed in the Library of Trinity College Dublin.[4] However, there is nothing to suggest a political association with what, by 1842, would be a long-dead claim to the throne. Perhaps Blayney Townley Balfour's motivation in purchasing the Jacobite items was partially provoked by the nineteenth-century romanticisation of the Jacobite saga, and the popularity of Walter Scott's *Waverley* (a number of Scott's works were also included in the Townley Hall library collection). There is, in any case, more work to be done on the fascinating figure of Blayney Townley Balfour, and his collecting inclinations and motivations.

Concluding Remark

The objects discussed in this paper were shown by projector on the day of the one-day seminar held at Europe house in Dublin to celebrate the tercentenary of Princess Clementina's dramatic liberation and escape. The rescue's success resulted in renewed Jacobite hopes for a Stuart succession and ultimate restoration to the thrones of Britain and Ireland. The marriage certificate of King James III and Queen Clementina is a testament to the aspirations of thousands of Irish, Scots and Englishmen who followed the Stuarts into exile until opportunity arose for a restoration of

4   Townley Hall and Townley Balfour family papers can be found in the National Library of Ireland, the Manuscripts and Archives Research Library of Trinity College Dublin, the Irish Architectural Archive, the UK National Archives and the British Library.

land, positions and kingdoms. Its ornate and striking beauty confirmed and communicated the prestige of Britain and Ireland's legitimate royal house to its adherents and political supporters across Europe during that time, but also across centuries to our own time. James II's *Book of Devotions* purchased by Blaney Townley Balfour is a direct connection to those who lived through the Williamite Wars and tells the story of a time when Irish identity encompassed a belief that the house of Stuart was the only legitimate house fit (indeed, divinely appointed!) to govern the kingdom of Ireland. This sense of identification with a British monarchy jars with the more recent conceptions of Irishness; but it was strong enough for thousands to take up arms against the Williamite usurper and to suffer death and exile for the ill-fated Stuart monarchy. Collectors like Townley Balfour have, through the artefacts they purchased, provided us with a window through which we can view a different Ireland and which informs our view of what it means to be Irish today.

Bibliography

Gittins, E., 'Jacobite relics in Trinity College, Dublin', in *History Ireland Magazine*, Vol. 26, No. 1 (January/February 2018).

Grosvenor, Bendor, 'The restoration of King Henry IX: identifying Henry Stuart, Cardinal York' *British Art Journal*, Vol. IX, No. 1, (spring 2008) <http://www.dnhdesign.com/BAJwebsite/BAJ-BG-HenryIX.pdf.>

Kelley, Bernard W., spelling, see above, *Life of Cardinal York*, 1899 (London and New York, 1899).

Papers of the Devotion of James II: being a reproduction of the Ms. In the handwriting of James the second now in the possession of Mr B.R. Townley Balfour with an introduction by Godfrey Davies (Roxburghe Club, Oxford, 1925).

With great thanks to the Very Rev. Robert Townley for discussions on the family history and Victoria Kavanagh for discussions on Townley Hall. Thanks also to Alison Palmer of Hever Castle and Gardens.

Contributors

Professor EDWARD CORP was Professor of British History at the University of Toulouse. He is a trustee of the Jacobite Studies Trust. He continues his prolific work on the Stuarts in exile which include *A Court in Exile: The Stuarts in France, 1689–1718* (Cambridge, 2004); *The Jacobites at Urbino: An Exiled Court in Transition* (Basingstoke, 2009); *The Stuarts in Italy, 1719–1766: A Royal Court in Permanent Exile* (Cambridge, 2011); and his latest publication, *Sir David Nairne: The Life of a Scottish Jacobite at the Court of the Exiled Stuarts* (Oxford, 2018).

DR DECLAN M. DOWNEY, lectures in European and in Japanese diplomatic history at University College Dublin. His research interests include the History of Diplomacy and International Law, Japanese-European relations, and Irish émigrés in Habsburg Europe (1600-1800). His extensive publications and leading role in major international research projects have been recognized with international honours and awards including the Austrian Order of Merit (2003), the Spanish Royal Order of Isabel la Católica (2008), and the Japanese Foreign Minister's Commendation (2020). In 2009, he became the first Irish citizen to be elected to membership of the Spanish Royal Academy of History (fd.1733). In 2018, he was appointed historical publications adviser to the Austrian Academy of Sciences. He served as a member of the Board of Trustees of Chester Beatty Library in Dublin Castle from 2012 to 2017.

MS ESTELLE GITTINS is an archivist and manuscripts curator in the Research Collections department of the Library of Trinity College

Dublin with responsibility for post medieval historical collections. She received her degree and postgraduate degrees from Warwick University, St Andrews University and University College Dublin. She joined the Library of Trinity College Dublin in 2005 after a decade working as an archivist in the museums, galleries and archives sector in the UK and Ireland including Christie's auction house and the National Gallery of London.

Professor MARY ANN LYONS, Chair of History at Maynooth University, is a specialist on Franco-Irish relations and Irish migration to continental Europe in the early modern period, and is particularly interested in Jacobite migrants in Paris, c.1690–c.1730. She has also published on various aspects of Irish history including the Kildare dynasty, religion in late medieval and early modern Ireland, women, and the emergence of professional medicine from the early 1600s onwards. She is currently working on a biography of Thomas Arthur, M.D., of Limerick.

MR RICHARD K. MAHER is a teacher of Gaeilge, politics, cultural and social history, and English as a second language at Rathmines College of Further Education in Dublin. He graduated from University College Dublin with a first-class MA in Irish Studies in 2013. The paper he delivered at the Second International Congress on Ireland and Iberian Atlantic in Seville in 2016 has recently been published. He took a significant part in the organisation of the public seminar held at Europe House on 30 April 2019 which celebrated the tercentenary of Princess Clementina's rescue and escape. His areas of interest include Irish émigré networks abroad, court studies and the Irish language.

DR ANETA MARKUSZEWSKA studied musicology and in 2003 graduated at the Warsaw University. In 2005 she graduated at the Frederic Chopin Academy of Music in Warsaw (harpsichord in a class of Władyslaw Kłosiewicz) and a year later in Hochschule für Musik in Würzburg (Historische Tasteninstrumente, class of Prof. Glen Wilson). Since December 2003 she is an assistant in the Department of Musicology at the Warsaw University. In July 2011 she received her Ph.D. based on her thesis titled Festa and music at the court of Maria Casimira Sobieska in Rome (1699–1714). She is interested in opera of seventeenth and eighteenthth centuries and keyboard, especially harpsichord music. Her publications concern music and society in seventeenth and eighteenth centuries.

DR ÉAMONN Ó CIARDHA is a Reader in the School of Arts and Humanities at the University of Ulster and has taught History, English and Irish at the University of Toronto, the Keough Institute for Irish Studies, University of Notre Dame, Trinity College Dublin, the University of the Saarland, the University of Vienna. His researches are primarily focused on Irish Jacobitism (Irish support for the exiled House of Stuart), the Irish outlaw, Irish military history, Irish popular politics and culture, language and literature and Irish book history. Major publications include *Ireland and the Jacobite Cause, 1685–1766. A Fatal Attachment* (Dublin, 2002; repr., 2004); (with David Finnegan and Marie-Claire Peters), *The Flight of the Earls: Imeacht na nIarlaí* (Derry, 2010); and (with Frankie Sewell and Alan Titley) *The Irish Book in Irish, 1567–2000s* (forthcoming, Oxford 2020).

DR JAROSŁAW PIETRZAK is a lecturer of modern European and Polish history with the Department of Modern History at the Pedagogical University, THEM. National Education Commission in Krakow. He graduated from the University of Łódź with a Ph.D. in 2014. He is a member of the Society for Court Studies in London, the Polish Historical Society and the Polish Society for Research of the Eighteenth Century. His areas of interest include Polish history, court studies and European history.

Index

Printed by
CPI books GmbH, Leck